Thomas Hall

The purity and destiny of modern spiritualism

Light for the seeker: Hope for the weary hearted

Thomas Hall

The purity and destiny of modern spiritualism
Light for the seeker: Hope for the weary hearted

ISBN/EAN: 9783337269333

Printed in Europe, USA, Canada, Australia, Japan

Cover: Foto ©Thomas Meinert / pixelio.de

More available books at **www.hansebooks.com**

THE PURITY AND DESTINY OF
MODERN SPIRITUALISM

Thos. B. Hall

✠ ✠

THE

PURITY AND DESTINY

OF

MODERN SPIRITUALISM

Light for the Seeker
Hope for the Weary Hearted

FROM THE PEN OF

THOMAS BARTLETT HALL

PUBLISHED BY

CUPPLES AND SCHOENHOF
128 TREMONT STREET, BOSTON, MASSACHUSETTS

✠ ✠

TWO COPIES RECEIVED.

First impression numbering 550 copies printed November, 1899.

MANUFACTURED BY CUPPLES & SCHOENHOF,
BOSTON, U. S. A.

Dedication.

TO THE

Master Builders

WITHOUT NAME AND UNSEEN OF MORTAL EYE,

WHO HAVE BEEN USHERING IN THE DAWN OF

The Wonderful Day

NOW OPENING, BUT EVER AND ONLY IN SERVICE OF

THE SPIRIT OF TRUTH, THIS LITTLE BOOK IS

Lovingly Inscribed.

✠   ✠

DAYBREAK.

"In vain
Ye call back the Past again,
The Past is deaf to your prayer!
Out of the shadows of night
The world rolls into light;
It is daybreak everywhere."

The Bells of San Blas.

INTRODUCTION.

As these "modern ghosts" will not "down" at the bidding of old science, nor yield to the anathemas of any established ecclesiasticism, but rather persist the more in demanding the attention of all classes, through their varied forms of manifestation, and their claim to be not the least potent, if not the principal factors in the great movements, social, political and religious, which are to-day agitating and revolutionizing the whole world of humanity, the writer of this little book once more, and in continuation of previous endeavors in this direction,[1] feels moved to do his part, so far as he may be able and permitted, in bringing the cause of Modern Spiritualism to

[1] "Modern Spiritualism by a Bible Spiritualist." — Boston: Crosby & Nichols, 1863.
"Modern Spiritualism, or the Opening Way." — Boston: A. Williams & Co., 1883.

the observation and study of the many sincere thinkers who are still holding themselves aloof; and perhaps to help those who
have entered upon the investigation to find
their way better.

Surely some quickening power has been
brought to bear upon human life everywhere
during the last fifty years, touching and
kindling into flame the refuse that has been
gathering out of human experience, and
bringing all earth life to judgment, while
plainly ushering in new conditions, higher
aspirations, broader philanthropies, which
every day seem more and more imminent.
In all his dealings with man, God works
through agencies which alone are within
man's developing comprehension, while He
is ever concealed behind the clouds in which
He is wonderfully wrapped from mortal
vision. May it not be that this opening of
the spirit spheres is part, and no small part,
in the varied instrumentalities for lifting and
reclaiming man out of the low grade of the
centuries long past, from which he is now
plainly emerging? These agencies from
the spirit spheres, high and low, as recognized by Spiritualists, have come in the
providence of God for far other purpose

than the mere amusement of wonder seekers. They are brought nearer and more effectually to earth life at the closing of an old and the opening of a new cycle in the planet's development, to quicken, to judge and be judged, but always through individual experiences: for as the kingdom of God is within each and all, so are the judgment seat and the retribution, whether on this or the other side of the veil of time.

Modern Spiritualism broke in upon human experience to find very mixed conditions of good and so-called evil; and dealing with these it could not be otherwise than that the first fruitage should be equally mixed. The time seems to have come for a winnowing of such fruits as have thus far appeared, and so there has been an apparent diminution of interest in the cause, leading outside observers "and some within the fold" to think that Spiritualism is dying out. The fact would rather seem to be that while the original centres of attraction and manifestation have appeared to be losing their adherents, in reality the interest is being diffused and extended by those who have seen the new light returning to their old associations, and sowing the seeds of the new unfolding

among them all. The results of such sowing will in time be seen, if not already apparent, in the general quickening which has
been manifested, and of which more may be
expected. The work will go on as directed
by the higher powers which have had it in
charge. Gradually the varied forms of
manifestation and different grades of mediumship will be brought to more systematized
relations, which will be marshalled and held
as a science worthy the attention and study
of mankind.

With all the interesting developments
attained to-day, the science of Modern Spiritualism is still in its infancy. Its relation to
distinctly religious interests, through its
bearing upon questions of conduct as affected by the conditions and requirements
reported of the spirit spheres, would seem
to have invited the special inquiry of those
who have been called to the offices of religion. But the whole body of such laborers
have been held by their education and habits
of mind in strange antagonism from the
time of the first simple sounds announcing
the spirit approaches, and are still apparently
more eager to hear that all Spiritualism is a
fraud, than to learn by patient inquiry what

it does mean, and for what end its advent has been providentially permitted.

Spiritualism is not to be taken as a culmination of man's uplifting, but is to be studied and understood as introducing new forces in the development of this planet and all life upon it. It does not mean, and plainly is not permitted to assume man's individual responsibilities : but would rather teach him to feel that upon him, as the head of the line, lies all the heavier requirement that he should rise, with his increasing opportunities and widening range of knowledge, toward the highest development of which he is capable. It is not of itself a new dispensation, but one of the opening ways in which mankind, on both sides of the veil, are bound to move on to the higher and better things of the near opening cycle; so that through it shall be fulfilled all the hopes and promises so long held out as man's rightful inheritance.

The mighty Energy by which the great principles of Love, Justice, and Truth were originally implanted in the earth sphere, knows no failure in their ultimate carrying out, though centuries have come and gone in which man has been learning that they cannot be gainsayed or thwarted except to his own destruction. Man must and will move on until at last he shall yield himself joyously to their beneficent direction and control. Then and not till then will peace on earth and good will prevail.

Of the nine Articles herein published the first three were given to the public in 1863, under the title of " Modern Spiritualism by a Bible Spiritualist." The second three were given in 1883, twenty years later, and called, " Modern Spiritualism, or the Opening Way." The three Articles now added at this close of the year 1899, make the third series, completing nine in all, and covering the writer's experience during the many years since his attention was first awakened to what seemed to him the most momentous topic that could be brought to the study and contemplation of man — the question which all must sooner or later meet — What of the after-life and that bourn whence it had been before maintained that " no traveller returns "? Taken as a whole, the Articles form a progressive treatment, sustaining and in a way illustrating each other, and for this reason they are brought together.

With no thought of assumption of knowledge which is not open to every sincere seeker, but with the conviction that his asking for bread has not been answered with a stone, the writer commits this little book to the thoughtful consideration of all truth seekers ; rejoicing to be of service if it may be to any, while ready and glad always to be shown a better way.

THOMAS BARTLETT HALL.

BOSTON, *November*, 1899.

CONTENTS.

ARTICLE I.

DAWN OF THE NEW DAY.

ARTICLE II.

HEART AND HEAD. — THEIR ANTAGONISM.

ARTICLE III.

SPIRITUALISM AND MATERIAL INTERESTS.

✠   15   ✠

Contents

Contents

✠   **Contents**   ✠

Contents

ILLUSTRATIONS.

NOTE.

The publishers deem it their duty to the author to state that the placing of the second of these portraits upon the title-page was done at their instance and not at his.

So placing them shows the countenance at a period when the earlier portions of the work were written in contrast with its present aspect of added years and experience.

✠ 19 ✠

THE PURITY AND DESTINY OF MODERN SPIRITUALISM.

First Series.

Father, I thank Thee! May no thought of mine
Swerve from the path of duty, and of love,
To Thee, and all mankind.
Help me to know Thee as Thou art,
Give me a loving true and faith-full heart,
Oh, let me do my humble part,
In serving Thee!

FIRST SERIES.

1863.

ORIGINAL PREFATORY NOTE.

In willing, but cautious obedience to promptings which have thus far led him to the beginning, and successful accomplishment, of many things, often small in themselves, but serving for an experience to strengthen his faith, the writer of these Articles has adopted this more permanent form for their publication; and he now sends them forth to the world, with an earnest prayer, that they may accomplish something of the good, for which alone, he humbly hopes, they have been written.

It seems proper to add, that the Writer has never been a reader of the leading productions of other pens upon the topics here treated. He has never read a word in the voluminous works of Swedenborg, or of any

of his disciples. Neither has he read any publication written by Spiritualists, except a few
poems, from the pen of the Rev. Thomas L.
Harris, and his school of Spiritualists. His
knowledge of Modern Spiritualism is wholly
from his own careful, earnest study and
search into its various phases, in a deep
conviction that there must be a mighty
truth concealed beneath all the strange phenomena, which would well repay the labor
of investigation. He speaks wholly out of
his own experience. How far he has been
repaid for his patient research, may perhaps
be left to the determination of the reader,
who is desired to peruse the articles carefully, in earnest seeking for the truth; and
especially to discover, and make known, any
hidden poison which so many conscientious
persons are ready to insist lies concealed in
any, the best possible phase, of Modern
Spiritualism.

The chief ends sought to be reached in
these Articles, are: — to show that there is a
true spirituality underlying the whole subject;—to point out briefly the conditions,
and explain the difficulties, which have made
necessary the otherwise strange method of
its development, out of which all the while

is working, in ways as yet little comprehended even by those who have been admitted into its deepest mysteries, the sure
fulfilment of things declared in the Scriptures;—then to show, by brief allusions,
the great wants of the modern Christian
Church, which cry aloud for something
that shall give a new impulse, a new life
to its stagnant faith;—and last, but not
least, to declare that Modern Spiritualism
has come, not to deny, but to confirm, not
to break down, but to strengthen and establish in our minds and hearts, the teachings of
the Holy Book, the inspired Word of God,
by a new inpouring of the Holy Spirit,
amounting, in its fullness, to a new Dispensation.

Thus the three Articles here published seem
to complete the preliminary presentation of
a subject, which will be exhausted only when
Time is lost in Eternity.

✠   ✠

THE PURITY AND DESTINY OF
MODERN SPIRITUALISM.

ARTICLE I.

Dawn of the New Day.

Opening Difficulties in the Inquiry. — Hume. —
Mahan's Exposition. — Mediumship. — Individuality. — Bible Student a helpful Medium. — Good
accomplished. — Old conditions tested.

" The hour cometh, and now is, when the true worshipper
shall worship the Father in spirit and in truth."

IT matters not whether we adopt the
theory that this globe has, from its infancy
to its present state, progressed out of chaos
by separate acts of creation, under the fiat of
the Almighty; or whether we believe that
the process of growth has been one of development out of the life principles so impressed upon the new world at its birth, that

time could not go on without their unfolding, gradually, according to a law. The
great fact is admitted by all, independently
of these theories of growth, that there have
been what are conveniently called creative
epochs in this world's history, which are
distinctly marked as divisions of time, though
their precise beginning and ending have
eluded the research of the best of our
science. There was a time, *we know*, when
this earth, now so beautifully clothed with
vegetation, was bare of all growing things.
So there must have been, and was, a time
when this vegetation began to creep over
the earth's surface. There was a time when
there was no animal life sustained by breath-
ing the earth's atmosphere, and there was a
time when animal life had its beginning.
There was a time, too, when man was not,
and a time when he began to people the
earth. These epochs have come gradually,
not only in reference to the whole process of
the earth's development, but, judging from
all we can learn by scientific investigation,
and from all analogy, each epoch has, in
itself, been the subject of a gradual introduction and growth, and a gradual decay
and disappearance as it has given way to its

succeeding epoch; or rather seems to have been the foundation on which the epoch succeeding has been built up. Each new epoch has sprung into being, not complete and full grown, but from germinal beginnings that have found their life and sustenance in the ashes of the past; each successive epoch furnishing, in its ashes, material for a higher growth in the scale of being.

These epochs have proceeded in regular series, and the last so-called act of creation was the coming of man. Of man's beginning we know nothing. Far back in the East we discern glimmerings of light upon the questions when and how the human race began its career upon earth; but they are merest glimmerings, and convey to us nothing more than the beautifully simple record of the Bible, that God created man in his own image, and he called their name Adam. Through what vicissitudes of life, what changes and varieties of condition, what growth and refinement, physical and spiritual, this race of beings has been brought to its present development, cannot be stated in any brief compendium. That this world is, however, progressing as heretofore, to some higher condition, and that the beings who are ultimately to inhabit it will rank higher in the scale than its present occupants, is inevitably inferred from all analogy, and is received by all Christians at least, if not by all civilized people, as an event which awaits only the sure fulfilment of prophecy.

No wise man will dare to say that, even in his lifetime, there may not be developments promising things yet to be, which were never dreamed of in his philosophy. We know not when to look for the signs of the coming great change, though we perhaps do know through the Christian dispensation, what the signs shall be, when the great change approaches. That it will be gradual, we argue from analogy, — that it will come silently, without proclamation, "like a thief in the night," we believe from revelation.

It is but a few years since the American public were surprised and amused with the tidings of what was first known as, the "Rochester Knockings." By most persons the story was entirely disbelieved, and deemed unworthy of a second thought, much less a sober consideration. From that little beginning, what a strange progress and development the thing called Spiritualism, be it true or false, has attained! Subjected to ridicule

the most sarcastic that could be invented ;
to examinations and tests of as various kinds
as there are variety of conceits in the human
brain ; explained, over and over again, by as
many different theories as learned minds to
examine, — theories frequently militating
against each other, so that the defender of
the cause can often find his best arguments
in the mouths of those who think to condemn ; the most educated classes of the
community, with old Harvard at their head,
arrayed in opposition ; the Church issuing
its anathemas against it with a bitterness that,
had it been sustained by public opinion,
would have brought the early votaries of
Spiritualism to a fiery stake ; little understood, often entirely misunderstood, used
and abused in every conceiveable way, still
the glaring fact remains, that no cause, moral
or intellectual, civil or religious, physical or
spiritual, ever made such progress in secur-
ing the attention, and the more or less enlightened faith, of men, as this same cause
of Spiritualism. Its active opponents seem
to have pretty much given up their fruitless
attempts to stop it, and have sunk back
from their labors, seeking consolation in the
thought, that, if it contained no truth, it

could not prevail; they have left it, where indeed they found it, in God's hands, to manage according to his own wisdom and high behest. The result is, as far as our observation goes, that the community is divided upon this subject into two large classes; namely, those who believe in Spiritualism, in the broad acceptation of the term, and those who do not believe it, but think there must, or may be, something in it. The number of those who utterly reject all its facts and phenomena as trickery, is too small to be named as a class.

Such a subject demands something more than an occasional notice from the pen of journalists, in the ordinary course of comment upon matters that may interest the public. It is, therefore, with no wish to write a passing criticism, or merely to offer a readable article, that we have undertaken to present our views upon Spiritualism; but from an earnest desire to help others to know something of a mighty cause, through the highways and byways of which we have been laboring in the search after truth. Like all pioneers, we have had our experience, which ought to be of value to those who may desire to know the truth like ourselves; and if we can point out any of the dangers, the rocks on which some poor mortal's bark might otherwise be wrecked, we shall feel that we have done some good, whilst we do humbly trust that, as we seek God's blessing on our work, there may be other more positive fruits of our labor. Perhaps what we have to write might be called, the "Confessions of a Medium;" not confessions of our own sins, though God knows we have fallen into errors enough, but confessions of the wonder-workings of an all-wise Father, who rules these things, as all others, — confessions of a deep experience, that has awakened our spirit to new life, and leads it to pray daily that it may be so privileged of God as to do its humble part in bringing his kingdom upon the earth, in seeing to it that his will be done here, even as it is done in heaven. We write what we do know, not what we have heard others tell of. We would be humble as a little child, seeking the truth, with God's blessing on our prayers.

It is about ten years, a little more (1855), since our acquaintance with Spiritualism began through Daniel Hume,[1] of whose medium

---

[1] Later known as D. D. Home.

qualities most persons have heard something. The subject was new then, and
people would not believe their senses. Upon
his departure for Europe, he was playfully
called "Hum-bug." But those who win
may laugh; his powers, whatever they were,
opened the way for him to the inner chambers of the man who, of all men of that day
and generation, has ranked, and still ranks,
the shrewdest, sharpest, the veriest juggler,
whom nobody would deceive, and whom
nobody could find out. This man, then
reigning Emperor of the French, with wit
and capacity to detect fraud equalled by
few, and with position and power to punish
it when detected, without appeal, did not,
could not, find the key to Mr. Hume's
wonder-workings, except in the explanation
which the phenomena have ever claimed for
themselves. Before his departure, we had
many opportunities of meeting Mr. Hume
in private circles and family gatherings,
which offered every chance for testing the
reality of the phenomena, so that we became
fully convinced that they were no ocular
delusion, no mistake of our senses, and perhaps might be, what they purported to be,
the works of spirit power. It is enough

here to say of them, that they combined a variety of physical manifestations, mind-readings, and what purported to be spirit communications, which is not often found in any one medium. He left us wondering; and we looked round for other proofs, other mediums, other experience.

Having advanced so far as to believe in the actuality of the phenomena, doubt not, reader, we soon found ourselves in a very sea of perplexities, and that we were often tempted to give up our inquiry in despair. But remembering that we were pioneers, we determined to brave all hazards, to meet all difficulties, for the sake of truth. Our first great trouble was, that we had ever attached to the word " Spiritualism " a sense of something high and holy; whilst we found neither in the mediums, nor in the phenomena, any special characteristic that marked the high, or the holy; for they partook of all degrees, from the highest of Heaven's blessed truths to the lowest of Hell's horrors. It seemed to us then that the wrong term had been used, and that it should have been Spiritism, or Demonism, in the original sense of demon. And this was, after all, the most natural; for if the good spirits could come to bless us, why could not the bad ones come to plague us ; or if the low could come, why not the high? God works by general laws and special providence, in Spiritualism, as in all other things.

Satisfied so far, still we found ourselves continually perplexed, sometimes beyond endurance, by the absurdities, the contradictions, the follies, nay, the wickedness, that broke out upon the community under the guise of Spiritism. With what gratitude did we receive the book published in 1855, by Rev. A. Mahan, President of Cleveland University, entitled, "Modern Mysteries Explained and Exposed." Weary and worn with our labors, ready to sink in the turmoil of doubts that surrounded us, we welcomed that explanation, incomplete though we knew it to be, as sufficient to furnish a retreat wherein we might at least have some rest. He did not pretend to deny the facts of the manifestations, which we knew could not be denied, and so gained our willing concession to his theory of "odilic force." It was sheer fatigue that enabled us to find any rest in this poor shelter ; but it sufficed to give us a moment's respite, only to renew the inquiry with increased earnestness, de-

termined, with our own good-will, and in
God's own time, to find the truth which we
felt assured must be waiting to rejoice those
who would strive after it. "Knock and it
shall be opened unto you," "Seek and ye
shall find," were blessed words of encouragement, which seemed to bring us a new
strength. Seeking the truth only for the
truth's sake, we trusted that God would
guide us, and guard us, through all our
deviations from the true path. We prayed
to him, that, if there were truth in these
things, we too might know, in our own experience, the mysteries of mediumship. We
asked that we might know in our own consciousness, through external or internal sense,
the actual presence of the spirit world about
us. At last the answer began to come. We
became sensible of slight touches upon the
head, as though a hand were gently passed
over it. We had not expected this manifestation, and at first doubted it; but frequent
recurrence of the sensation, often under circumstances that caused us much surprise,
proved that it was not the work of our
imagination, but a real touch from some
body or thing, some power or spirit, that
thus informed us of its presence, and was

perhaps communicating some mysterious influence.

It is unnecessary to describe the stages of development through which we have passed. Suffice it to say, that, though yet far short of the goal, if indeed there be any limit, we have been carried, sometimes quite imperfectly, into enough phases of mediumship to give us an understanding of all these things from our own experience. Each day as we have advanced, the importance of prayer has been urged upon us, and we have felt its power wonderfully in guiding our search for truth, and saving us from the errors committed by others who have not known the wonder working of a true appeal to the Great Father of all spirits. Especially have we been saved from too rapid development, which has so often led men to commit follies that have brought ridicule, and sometimes disgrace, on the very cause they had most at heart. In this, as in all other subjects that may interest and occupy the human mind, too much, or too sudden knowledge, topples the reason, and opens the way for folly to enter in. We have often thanked God in gratitude for the reply made through a medium to our earnest prayer for development: "You shall have the truth as fast as you can bear it; for if it should come as fast as it could be given, it would craze your brain."

We have spoken of passing through certain stages of development *imperfectly*. By this we learned that, whilst such forms of mediumship have their use, particularly for the purpose of introducing Spiritualism to the world's notice, they are not the highest forms. We believe that the highest form of mediumship is that where the individuality of the medium is the most developed and the most active, so that the medium's self, being a spirit in the body, may draw directly from the spiritual fountains of God's eternal truth and power, as mankind has generally believed the spirits of the departed would be privileged to do, according to their spiritual deserving and capacity. In other words, the highest mediumship is what has been heretofore vaguely known as *inspiration*, and sometimes called *genius*. We mean inspiration in its broadest sense, in every kind of knowledge to which the human mind has been permitted to give expression. Religious inspiration, in its various phases; the inspiration of the fine arts, music, poetry, painting, sculpture; the inspiration of the mechanic arts in all the phases of invention; the inspiration of the philosopher; the inspiration of what is often called plain common-sense. They all flow from the same source, — God's great fountains of knowledge. As Solomon said, there is nothing new under the sun. All knowledge exists in spirit life before man slowly elaborates it for external expression on this earth plane, and the degrees of so-called genius are marked by the varying capacity to receive and express it. This idea is involved in the word *impression*, so often used by men in their every-day business affairs. They have "impressions" so and so; sometimes against the convictions of their reason. Where do these impressions come from? What are they? They are the result of influences from spirit life that surround every human being, that "cloud of witnesses," of which we read in Scripture; and they will be of a higher or lower character, exactly according to the spiritual condition of each individual. God works through agents more or less directly. The spirits in the spirit world are the messengers which bear tidings of good, and of so-called evil, to every one according

to his desire and capacity to receive. As
this desire and capacity to receive depends,
under God's blessing, upon each individual
will, so each one of us has to work out his
own salvation in very truth. But not without aid : the power of prayer is mighty ; the
Father of spirits will send us such influences
as we truly ask for. Ask, and ye shall
receive,— even the desired presence of the
blessed spirit of Jesus.

This principle of individuality is one of
the most important teachings of Spiritualism,
though, we admit, nothing in itself new, and
offers, at the same time, the simple explanation of one of the serious difficulties in the
way of the public acceptance and acknowl-
edgment of the reality of spirit presence and
power. It is the first and last objection of
the educated classes, that Spiritualism has
given to the world so little, if anything, *new*
in science, or indeed in any of the ordinary
matters that have heretofore occupied the
educated mind. It is true that very little
has been given to common mundane science,
in distinct propositions, through ordinary
mediumistic communications, and it is for
the reason, now beginning to be understood,
that when God permits the spirit world to

draw close to the earth life, he does not
intend that the spirits out of the form shall
assume all the responsibilities, do all the
thinking, perform all the labors, bear all the
burdens, of those in the form. Such a
course, if permitted, would have directly
taken away man's accountability ; his individuality would be gone ; and so experience
has taught very many inquirers that they
cannot long act with safety in matters of
worldly interest under the sole direction of
mediumistic communications. The cause
of Spiritualism has seemed to suffer, as unbelievers have had opportunity to point the
finger of ridicule at the sad and absurd errors
committed by Spiritualists, who have been
working out this result of their experience,
earning this wisdom for their own, and the
world's benefit. It is only when the medium's own spirit is developed, so as to
receive impressions direct, that he can with
safety act them out through his own enlightened mediumistic consciousness ; but even
then the promptings must ever be brought
to the bar of conscience, God within us ;
whilst the reason must sit in external judgment to determine pure questions of external
prudence and policy. We must ever, as St.

Paul says, "try the spirits," that we "may prove them."

At the risk of some repetition, we will endeavor to explain more clearly what may perhaps be called the philosophy of mediumship. When the man of so-called genius finds new ideas crowding into his brain, it cannot be said that he makes them. All the result of the scholar's study is to bring the mind into condition to receive the thoughts that are ever waiting for admission, when the mind is ready and able to accept and comprehend them. It is no mere play of fancy, when the poet begins his labor with an invocation to the muses. It is an act of preparation, to lift the poet's spirit into a condition to receive the poesy that is ready to flow in upon him. The most hard-headed philosopher must be in what he would call, the right spirit, or he cannot think (receive thoughts) effectively. A genius, then, and there are as many kinds of genius as subjects to occupy the human mind, is the medium through whom the ideas floating in the spirit world, existing in the spirit life, are given external expression, so as to be more or less comprehended by the minds of others. The man of genius gives expression to the thoughts which are given to him, and commits them to paper. They are printed in a book. This book in turn becomes the medium for the transmission of the ideas to the ordinary reading minds, which, on their part, must be developed to a condition able to receive the ideas, or the words read are hieroglyphics without meaning. The man of genius gets the ideas by inspiration from the world of spirit; the ordinary man of talent must wade through the printed pages, and receive the same ideas by slow induction, word by word. Precisely as the man of genius receives, and gives expression to the ideas which are given to him, so Spiritualism teaches us, truth is handed down by gradation from the central fount of eternal knowledge and truth, through the various conditions of spirits in the spirit world, who progress and rise from one to another of those " many mansions," each nearer to the source of direct inspiration.

Now spirit mediums, as commonly recognized, are supposed, by outside observers, to be the mere instruments used, or purporting to be used *wholly* by *other spirits* for purposes of manifestation and communication. The fact is that there are all degrees of mediumship, from this entire absence of the

medium's self, to the complete inspiration,
where the medium's consciousness and individuality are in full action. They are mediums in this latter case as much as in the
former; the difference being that, in the latter case, the medium's own spirit uses its own
organism to express the inspiration which is
given to it more or less directly, whilst in the
former case, another spirit controls the medium's body, and is itself the communicator
of thoughts, to which it has been receptive,
and now seeks to express. We believe that
those mediums will give to the world the
most new things, and the highest truths,
whose individuality is never lost, and is in
the highest state of development. Of course
those forms of mediumship which only afford
tests of spirit presence, resulting in the identification of friends who have passed on, are
desirable, if not indispensable, to satisfy the
preliminary inquiries of those who begin by
being either curious, or anxious, to know
whether the world of spirits is really so near
this earth as it professes to be. But these
tests are given quite independently of any
consideration of the medium's own development. Indeed, the most remarkable tests
sometimes have come through those of low

condition, physically and spiritually. These
tests are given in a great variety of forms.
A very striking form is in the appearance of
the names of departed ones, in letters of red
on the arm; a phenomenon which has as-
tounded many hundreds of persons, as shown
in two mediums recently in Boston. This
class of mediums has been, and still is, essential to the introduction of Spiritualism to
man's notice and comprehension,— it began
with table tipping and rapping, the first rude
alphabet of communication,— it will disappear when it has done its work. Already
many mediums who have been used only for
tests are losing their powers, or falling off
into neglect.

Let it not be supposed, however, that the
tendency of Spiritualism is solely to intellectual development and manifestation. In accordance with the spirit of this age, it has
found its introduction to the world's notice,
in a great degree, through the intellectual faculties and purely intellectual observations.
It could not have been introduced in any
other way to a people like the American
nation, which had become so eager in the
pursuit of material prosperity through intellectual development, that the nation's heart

has needed its present fearful awakening under the hands of an all-wise Providence, which, in our belief, is but the beginning of a mighty struggle for dominion between the powers of good and the powers of evil, that is yet to sweep over the face of the whole globe. This consideration leads us to the higher, or what in common acceptation would be deemed, the more spiritual development of Spiritualism, which is now gradually unfolding to the wonder and delight of all its truest advocates.

Whilst it is admitted that an equal development of heart and head are necessary to make the perfect man, we believe that the heart must be first cultivated, or the head cannot receive true wisdom. Without an understanding of the heart, the knowledge of the head is full of errors that lead the spirit to its ruin. This is no new proposition; the philosophy of it is simple. True heart development brings that *peace* of mind which fits it, the mind, for the highest intellectual conceptions, makes it receptive to the highest truths. Yet the nations who boast of their Christian civilization have ignored it, and set up intellectual idols that have received their souls' devotion for six days in every week, and been hardly forgotten in the midst of their would-be sacred observance of the seventh. Wonderful has been the intellectual and material progress of the nations, and particularly of this people, during the past century; but is it not true that spiritual culture and development have been retarded, if not retrograded, in the same degree? Witness the practical results; see, for example, the utter selfishness of the trading, commercial classes. With few exceptions, every man of them is striving, with his whole soul, to find out, *not* how he can help his neighbor, but how he can get ahead of him. Alas, for such Christian followers! We fear the Founder of their religion would hardly recognize his disciples among them. But this is no place for a homily upon the sins of the nations. We should shrink from such a task under any conditions; to catalogue them only would be a fearful undertaking, for their name is legion.

The feeling that true Spiritualism should have something, if not everything, to do with the understanding of the heart; and the fact that it has thus far, to the view of external observers, seemed to have so little to do with it, has been one great cause of the severest opposition it has experienced. For reasons which we shall hereafter endeavor to state, it appears to us to have been necessary, in the present condition of the world's development, that the near approach and communion of the spirit-world should be brought to the knowledge of mankind in the way it has been. Believing, as the Christian world professes to believe, in the second coming of Jesus, how many are there who would be able to recognize him now in our streets in the humble garb of the Nazarene? The difficulties are immense in the introduction of any really new phase in the world's development, arising out of the conditions of head and heart, into which such new development must gradually work its way. We are able now to see the wisdom that directed events, when the infant Jesus was laid in a manger, he "the Prince of Peace," "the Saviour of the world." As time goes on, the wisdom will be recognized which has directed the course of Spiritualism to its present unfolding, itself but the germ of what is yet to be.

We have spoken of our own continuous and unsatisfactory search after true spiritual mediumship, in the first years of our inquiry.

We did not feel that we had arrived at the
beginning of the truth, until we made the
acquaintance of a medium who had been
developed as such after an anxious study of
the Bible. This was a young person, born
of true New England parentage, in one of
the best of New England homes, of large,
healthful physique, with fine intellectual
powers, a broad head and large understanding, who had been drawn into the cause
against external convictions, as well as the
wishes of family and friends ; but who could
find happiness in no other direction, and
alone, before God, trusting the inmost dictates of the still small voice, after many
struggles, much wrestling with the spirit, had
determined to go forward with the work,
whatever it might be, so long as it did not
militate with the highest sense of right and
duty.

This person, called a healing and developing medium, was not under the control of
those who purported to be our relatives, or
particular friends in the spirit world, but
was wholly influenced by a few choice spirits,
who announced, through their unconscious
trance possession, that their medium had
been selected as an instrument of great good

to the world. What that good was, we did
not at first understand; we had yet to learn
it. The communications were addressed
wholly to our physical and spiritual condition, and the work of regeneration that was
to be done amongst the people. They were
not given in tedious homilies, but came in
quiet, natural suggestions, warnings, and
advice, accompanied at times with a manipu-
lation of the head, which had a strange sooth-
ing, yet invigorating power, easily and early
recognized. It was indeed a healing power,
and imparted a pure vitality, which by a
mysterious process gradually reached the
spirit within, and we felt that the old heathen
maxim of "sound mind in a sound body,"
had a spiritual meaning beyond its ordinary
acceptation. By slow degrees we began to
perceive the refined influence that seemed
to rain down upon our heads as we sat in
silent waiting. Not knowing what to expect,
the light of Heaven gradually illumined our
heart, and we were ready to acknowledge
that we could perceive a spiritual influx, as
we sat for development, which seemed to
give us, or itself to be, the true riches of
which the Scriptures teach, for it brought
with it, in very truth, that peace which

passeth all understanding. This is no idle fancy of our own, no mere play of the imagination; others have known it as well as we; it is difficult to describe or explain, but when realized by experience, brings with it a sense of reality such as nothing else seems to give. It seems almost the only reality of life.

At intervals the spirits, through this medium, would reason with us, as Paul, of righteousness; but whenever we asked for tests, such as are given through other mediums, they refused, for the reason that it would be a waste of powers which were dedicated to higher uses, as we have above endeavored to explain. We did not, we could not, accept the full meaning of this at once. Tempted in our progress to pursue comparatively idle inquiries, our prayers, and the kind words of the medium, saved us from dallying by the way-side. Purely intellectual investigation seemed to be for a time forbidden. Our business was with the heart alone. To purify that, to become as a little child, to sit at the feet of Jesus, and receive from his hands something of the Christ-spirit with which he was filled, this was our work, this the present object of life. It was (and is) a realization of the patriarch's dream, in which the angels,

God's messengers, are eternally ascending
and descending, bearing up to the throne the
petitions of His creatures, and bringing back
the responses of His mighty love,— responses which teach us to throw away selfishness utterly ; to live and labor for others ;
to dispense widely unto all ; to give freely,
as we have freely received, these treasures of
God's love ; to so explain these things, and
illustrate them in our lives, that they shall
show forth His goodness and glory.

These lessons could not be learned till we
had given up our conceit of knowledge obtained through purely intellectual culture ; and
now, humbled as a child before God, but a
man amongst men, we feel ready to begin a
good work, rejoicing that we find the yoke so
easy, the burden so light.

If we are asked, how can these things be
known to all, we say to all, high and low, rich
and poor, learned and unlettered, gather your-
selves in small circles, two or three together,
cheerfully, but soberly, reverently, in the
name of Jesus, pray for the light you need,
and it shall be given to you.   Let as nearly
as possible the same persons meet at each
successive gathering ; let the surroundings be
fit for such communion.   If the circle be in

a family,— and where better can it be ? — let
the place in the house be selected which is
freest from contaminating influences. It
would be well for the world if there could be
a " holy of holies " in every dwelling-house,
where the best influences could be poured
down upon those in waiting. Let not the
father of the family, the man of business, object that it will interfere with his daily avocations ; it will rather give him new strength for
all his duties. It is not for the Sabbath only,
but every day in the week ; whilst it teaches
still the true value and use of the great day
of rest. But chief of all, let not the man of
education, of learning, fancy that his time for
study cannot be interrupted for these things.
Let him rather forget his pride of intellect,
and an humble member of the circle, let him
ask for that true light which will illumine his
soul, and send its quickening rays into the
most hidden corners of his deepest researches.
It was in the highways that Jesus found his
first believers and disciples ; — must it be so
still ?

But be assured, that to follow these things
with trifling curiosity is to expose one's self to
the penalties of sacrilege. By laws to which
we have referred, you will get just what you

seek after. Beware lest you bring to the inquiry too careless a heart, or a head too vain
of its understanding. Do not, however,
think that you can turn away and neglect
these things for one motive or another with
impunity. Your likes or dislikes cannot
change the orderings of Providence. If the
near approach of the spirit world be a fact,
then it remains a fact whether you like it or
not. On the other hand, if it be true that
these influences, for good or for evil, are
around about, and so near you, it behooves
you to understand their powers and mode of
action, lest in your wilful ignorance you suffer approaches to which you would not know-
ingly be subject. In familiar phrase, if you
wish to know what company you keep, ever
influencing your feelings, your thoughts,
your actions, sometimes much more than the
friends and companions seen by your body's
eye, look closely into your heart, for as that
is, so shall your unseen companions be.
You cannot escape it. Understand yourself rightly, make yourself what you know
you ought to be, and you will learn to thank
God for the sweet angel influences that guide
and guard you through every hour of your
life.

Let not Spiritualism be rejected by outside observers, because they cannot see any
good yet accomplished by it. Misunderstood as it has been, much silent good has
been done that is not proclaimed aloud to the
world. By it many doubting minds have been
established in a faith in the future life of the
spirit; whilst many more have been relieved
of the most depressing fears of the everlasting retribution, the relentless eternity of
punishment, by learning that progress is the
law of God's universe in the spirit world, as
in the earth life; and the blessed consolation
of a divine hope has given them new courage
to try to attain a higher, better, holier condition, according to their capacity, and not
according to the dogmas of their theology.
Still more good has been wrought out of
Spiritualism, through the very errors of its
early converts. Good has come out of the
wrongs committed under the name of Spiritualism, by showing the sad inefficiency of the
Christian Church of this day. We say it
not in unkindness, but in sadness; we say it
not of any particular denomination or sect:
it is true of all, as out of all have come those
unhappy victims of their own weakness, who
have, in the name of Spiritualism, thrown

off the cloak of religious observances under which they had concealed the rottenness of their hearts from the world's knowledge, if not from their own, and, availing of the assumed authority of false teachers and prophets, have in their actions confessed their little faith. It is a fearful proof of the want of true Christian grace, of vitality in their faith, that so many professors of the religion taught by Jesus, have been so easily led astray. Let them not make recantations, and lay the blame on Spiritualism, for it is but their own sins which have found them out; they may rather thank God that anything has come to show them their spiritual condition.

Angels are about us, the spirit world has, in this nineteenth century, been brought near to the earth life to mingle its influences for good, or for evil. Not, as it would seem, by an entirely new law; for these things have been before; but to an extent, and in a manner, which indicate, and are proclaimed as showing, a new dispensation in the providence of God. Exactly what this new dispensation will unfold is not for man to know yet, but that it is ushering in one of those great epochs in the progressive history of the earth

and its creatures, to which we have in the beginning referred, we do believe. Far be it from
us to presume to reach too far into the plans
of the Almighty ; but it is our solemn conviction, that these things do announce that
second coming of which the Scriptures teach.
The condition of the earth and its people,
the signs of the times, indicate this more than
ever before ; whilst the near presence of the
spirit world brings with it holy influences
which must elevate and spiritualize all of
earth's creatures who will receive them, and,
as good is ever stronger than evil, will, sooner
or later, drive off-into outer darkness all who
wilfully reject and oppose them out of the
ignorance, or the wickedness, of their hearts.
*If God's holy angels can and do so come, why
may not the blessed spirit of Jesus come too?
Has he not come already? Is he not in the
midst of us even now, and we know him not?*

May, 1862.

ARTICLE II.

HEART AND HEAD — THEIR ANTAGONISM.

Origin, growth and present state of antagonism between intellectual and spiritual culture. — The old
church and its short comings.

" Behold, I make all things new."

HAVING endeavored to show that there is
a true spirituality underlying the external expression of Modern Spiritualism, we would
now try to remove the chief obstacle which
has prevented many conscientious persons
from finding out this inner life, by explain-
ing the origin, growth, and present state of
the antagonism between intellectual, and pure
spiritual culture. This branch of the inquiry
may not be interesting to all readers, but we
deem it indispensable that it should be thor-
oughly examined, and fully comprehended,
before the more educated part of the community, as a whole, can be in condition to

receive the truth. We would reiterate, that
we write wholly from a desire, under God's
blessing, to give to others the light which
has been given to us ; understanding that
what we have to say cannot of itself persuade,
but only make others receptive to the *influences* which God is ready to pour in upon all
who will open themselves to the *"flowing in
of his spirit of love and truth."*

Nothing is more marked in the history of
opinion, whether relating to the commonest
interests of every-day life, or to the most
abstruse problems of scientific or metaphysi-
cal inquiry, than the disposition of mankind
to incline to extremes ; on the one side in
their tenacity of things already established,
and on the other side in their correction of
acknowledged errors. Discovering their
mistakes slowly, men are apt to adopt views
directly opposite to the old ones, and for
that reason full of new error. Whether this
arises from a laudable desire to find the truth,
and hold it firmly when discovered, or whether it has its origin in man's weak conceit,
leading him to assume the right and power
to fix the limits of knowledge, and declare
out of his own mouth the law, to the conception of which he has slowly attained, are

questions which we believe might be carefully
considered with much profit to self-sufficient
humanity. The fact is admitted by all ; and
the leaders in these opposite positions are
deemed the extremists of their time, and
properly so considered, whether they are on
the side of progress or conservatism. Few,
however, are able, though recognizing the
fact, to attain a position nearer to the truth ;
whilst most are content to flatter themselves
by pointing out the extreme views of others,
and pronouncing judgment on them even to
foolishness.

Of all extremists none are so unhappily
placed, at least for their own advantage, as
those who are on the side of conservatism ;
their case is almost hopeless. The extremists of reform are ever moving on to new
thoughts and new life ; making mistakes
enough in their self-anointed conceit, but
still getting lessons in their experience which
their conceit would not let them learn by the
gentler processes prepared by God for the
teaching of those his children who are willing
to humble themselves first before him, in
prayer for such light as he will vouchsafe to
give them in his own time, and in his own
way. Alas for the extremists of conservatism!

They never try to rise; they wish for nothing
new, no matter how much for the better.
They remain, as they suppose, firmly fixed
on everlasting truth; till suddenly they discover that the foundation on which they
rested has rotted away, or become too weak
for the superstructure; and from being the
most comfortably secure, they find themselves the most uncomfortably insecure of all
the world. Inevitably they either float off
without sails, without rudder, without compass, into a turbulent sea of doubt and dis-
traction; or, as the old ties give way, they
swing violently to the other and directly opposite extreme, yielding themselves to a
mixed rule made up largely of temper and
selfish chagrin, though its true character may
be concealed from themselves by their declared and acknowledged desire to do as
nearly right as they can. Their motive may
seem to be good; but they were extremists
in their conservatism, and they are become
extremists in their new light. We have remarkable instances of this in the political relations of the American people at the present
time, when the most ultra conservatists give
expressions to violent sentiments which fairly
leave behind many of those whom they form-

erly decried as dangerous, if not unprincipled reformers. The same thing may be seen in all the relations of life, if we will observe them carefully, even in the most insignificant matters.

It is not to be expected that men should be otherwise affected, and experience shows that they are not, in matters regarding their religious and spiritual interests. A few centuries ago, the civilized world was wholly subjugated to the Church, which had usurped to itself all authority over the minds and hearts of men, so that both in mind and heart man's individuality was lost. In knowledge of temporal things he became a child; and whenever the spirit world and its influences came near him, he fell at once into blind superstition, which culminated, at different intervals among the nations, in the various phases and terrors of witchcraft.

This assumption of the Church, arrogating to itself all knowledge, all power, in things temporal, and in things spiritual, though under the name of spiritual rule only, led to the Reformation of the seventeenth century. Breaking from the thraldom in which he had been held, man rushed into the arena which he found world-wide,—nay,

limited only by the limits of his own capacity. Not all at once did he obtain freedom from church rule. Even now it is far
from complete in things purely spiritual; for
the dogmatic theology of Protestantism has
at times held, and does in some directions
now, well-nigh hold, in spiritual things, the
very supremacy which led to the outbreak
of the seventeenth century. But the old impulse, the return pendulum-swing of opinion
started by the Reformation, continues; and,
believing that the old error was, in yielding
a blind obedience to the rule of those who
pretended to act wholly under spiritual guidance, and thus made distrustful of all things
purely spiritual and cognizable first, if not
wholly, by the heart, man still is, as he has
been, for the last two or three centuries,
going to the other extreme, and letting intellectual forces take the lead and control of
his development. The result is a disposition
to doubt everything not the subject of absolute independent intellectual conception, and
this has led, in different nations and at different periods, to conditions fatal to his highest spiritual development. In France, it
reached a climax in the fearful reign of Reason, and the bloody scenes of her great Rev-

olution. Throughout all Europe it has resulted often in a miserably unspiritual, if not
wholly Godless materialism. In our own
country the tendency has been to a materialism, not Godless, but wholly unspiritual.
The intellectual conception of the God principle has been retained, and he has been permitted to reign abstractly through such laws
as science has been able to investigate; but
he has been a God of the head only, not of
the heart. The tendency has been to recognize his power in the world's creation, and
perhaps in the daily orderings of the world's
life, but to ignore and deny the possibility
of a spiritual relation between man and his
Creator, other than man's ever-varying conceptions of his attributes.

In struggling to escape from the thraldom
of the old church, man has succeeded so far
as to be no longer subject in temporal things,
and to a great extent in spiritual things, to
its dominion. We see comparatively little
of the old superstitious relation between the
priest and the people. But in denying
the authority of the Church, and exercising
his own thought upon spiritual things, man
has been carried to the opposite extreme of
independence, and come to rely wholly on

his own strength, forgetting that there was a God behind the Church, whose power, whose love, the Church had arrogated to itself, and therefore lost its influence. Nay, the individual man has fallen into the very error which has led to the destruction of the Church's power, and constituted himself as the Church, with all knowledge, all power. As surely as the Church has lost its high position and power, so surely must individual man be humbled before the true, the only Church, which is of Christ. "It may or may not be a matter of regret," said an observant preacher, recently, "that church organizations seem to be crumbling; the great fact is left, that, where two or three are gathered together in the true Christ spirit, there will always be a true Church." He might have added, there only has the true Church ever been.

Still, progress is the law; and from this extreme intellectual development has come the power to resist the tendency to superstition in spiritual things which was almost unavoidable during man's thraldom to the Church,— a power without which he would not have been able to bear the recent advent of spiritual phenomena. The want of this power is even now shown in many individuals, who from mere fear are unable to approach the subject of Spiritualism, as presented in the more striking physical manifestations, though few are bold and truthful enough to themselves and their fellows to acknowledge their weakness. The old church superstition is not all worked out of them, though they little suspected it till these recent strange things forced them to show the fact in their actions, if not in words. A few of these timid ones try to persuade themselves that their fear is a proper fear of trenching upon sacred ground, an unwillingness to pry into the things upon which God has set the seal of mystery. But these either deceive themselves as to the fact, or their feeling is but another form of the old superstition which taught that the priest alone could know the ways of God. Let them remember that Christ died for all men, and to all men is it given to penetrate the very depths of spiritual things, if they will become worthy to be so blessed. To him that asketh, if it be in the right spirit, it shall be given. To him that knocketh in the name of Jesus, it shall be opened.

Believing, then, that out of this intellectual freedom has come to most men of this day and generation the ability to bear the approach of spirit phenomena, so far as to examine them without falling into the old superstition of witchcraft, we would endeavor to show more particularly how this has been brought about; to explain the working of the elements of head and heart, mind and spirit, which have heretofore held such antagonistic relations, and thus to reach, if we can, the true philosophy of this branch of the subject. We ask the candid reader's careful attention.

Thought and spirit are real things. They have substance, refined, as compared with material things, even up to sublimity; still they are real, substantial existences. It is difficult for us to come to a conception of this idea, this fact; and perhaps it is sufficient for the present to recognize them only as forces, of substance too ethereal and sublimated to be recognizable by the senses of the body, yet living forces. Now it cannot be denied that, since the Reformation of the seventeenth century, it has been the ever-increasing tendency of Protestantism to give unlimited sway and supremacy to intellect, and to reject all phenomena, all manifestations, which could not be discerned through the ordinary avenues of intellectual conception, and recognized through the ordinary channels of external sense. Thus, by the deliberate exercise of his will, the forces of man's intellect have been held in direct and successful opposition to the forces of his inner or spiritual life. The idea of spiritual discernment, as understood in the days of the Apostles, has been utterly repudiated, as having no possible place in our wise-thinking heads, and any suggestion of such a possibility in these days utterly rejected. Here is a plain, direct antagonism between subjects of external intellectual conception, and things of the spirit, to be spiritually discerned. From this antagonism has arisen the difficulty, especially of educated people, in receiving spirit manifestations, whether of the purer and more refined, or of the grosser kinds ; there being as many degrees of refinement among spirits, as mansions to receive them in the spirit world. The more men have been educated in the schools of the day, the greater has been their difficulty as regards these spiritual things. Too great confidence in their intellectual acquirements, or, to speak in plain terms, though not in unkindness, their self-reliant intellectual conceit, has repelled, or made impossible, all direct approaches from the spirit world. Herein we find the key to what has heretofore been considered the mystery of faith. There are three conditions to which the idea of faith has relation. First, entire disbelief; second, indifference as to belief, or mere willingness not to reject; and, third, active belief. In these three conditions are the three degrees: first, direct antagonism of the intellectual forces against the spiritual forces; second, a mere suspension of hostilities, with more or less of a guard to watch the enemy; and, third, the open receptiveness, the glad welcome to all the gifts and graces of the spirit, with all their accompanying blessings as they are worked out into external, or more material expression, on the earth plane.

There is no new law in these conditions. It prevailed equally in those early days when the Holy Spirit was manifested on earth in the form of Jesus. It was amongst the ignorant fishermen that he, the Nazarene, the carpenter's son, found his first disciples; simple-minded men, who had nothing to unlearn, and little, if any, intellectual antagonism to overcome. The educated men of

his day would not receive him. To the fishermen it was enough for him to say, " Follow
me,"— whilst it required a miraculous intervention to reach the heart of Paul. So, too,
in the more external workings and expression
of the spirit power, what might be called
the more physical manifestations of spirit,
wrought out through Jesus, the same law
prevailed ; and we are told in the Scripture
record, that the want of faith, or rather
their active disbelief, the intellectual antagonism, prevented a certain district of the
Jewish people from beholding the wonder-
workings of the miraculous power. Οὐκ ἐδύ-
νατο ἐκεῖ οὐδεμίαν δύναμιν ποιῆσαι, εἰ μή, etc., "And
he could there do no mighty work, save,"
etc. ; *was not able to do* is the literal transla-
tion, as it is the only meaning of the original Greek, though commentators find great
difficulty in accepting it, because of the
standpoint from which they take their view.[1]

By this same law of antagonism between
mind and spirit power, have many persons
been utterly prevented from witnessing even
the grossest forms of spirit manifestation in

[1] Gospel according to Mark, chap. vi. verses 5 and 6; also
Matthew, chap. xiii., verse 58. See note to this last verse in
Barnes's Notes on the Gospels.

these latter days. Learned men, relying on the education of their heads, have again and again endeavored to hear even the simple rappings with more or less conscious desire and will, not to find out what the strange thing was, but to prove that it was not what it purported to be; and they have gone away reassured in their wisdom of this earth, which in such an inquiry is indeed very " foolishness."

In obedience to this same law, there was a gradual disappearance, and latterly, up to the commencement of the rappings, there has been a remarkable cessation of all the manifestations, which in the days of church rule resulted in superstition and witchcraft. Appearing at intervals in the gradual decline of the Church's power, the fact of this final entire cessation has always been to our minds, until recently, quite inexplicable. Here and there, to be sure, we had heard of what were called haunted houses, and we had read of the Wesley rappings; but our education had taught us to consider all such things as manifestations of anything but spirit power, and most probably as the result of deluded imaginations. Still, Mansfield on the English bench, and Sewall on this side, had soberly sat in judgment, and had condemned on the evidence ; and the alternative has been either to deny the facts and stultify Mansfield and Sewall, as indeed we believe Sewall, later in life, did for himself; or to admit the facts in some way, and wonder why such things had so entirely disappeared in modern times. We now understand that this cessation of spirit manifestations has been owing to the power of mental forces, held by the will in antagonism with the spirit forces.

Let it be supposed, then, for the sake of the argument, if the position cannot otherwise be admitted by our readers, that, in the fullness of time, the period had come when the spirit world was moved through its depths to draw near to the earth life. How could it, under the condition of things which we have endeavored to explain, how could it signify its approach and near presence ? It has often been objected to modern spirit phenomena, that their method of expression is so mundane, so unspiritual, though claiming to be of spirit origin. The objectors have demanded that the spirits should come with gentler approaches, and in more ethereal guise. But it must be remembered that spiritual things, in what may be termed their more natural expression, can only be spiritually discerned; and how, we would ask, could these spiritual things be discerned by a race who utterly repudiated the possibility of such a manifestation, and deemed such an idea foolishness? Nay, how could the spiritual world even come near enough to be spiritually discerned by a people who were all the time repelling it, by the antagonism of which we have spoken? A little reflection shows that it was only through material signs, to be recognized by the senses of the material body, that the spirit world could begin to effect any approach. It was because the world in the flesh was deaf to the still small voice, that resort to the gross, or material manifestations, by rappings, was necessary. Even these manifestations owed part of their influence to, if they were not necessarily preceded by, the phenomena of mesmerism or animal magnetism, to the laws of which recourse has so often been had for an explanation of the spirit phenomena, which otherwise would have compelled many minds to admit that they were what they purported to be. Thus gradually, through the three degrees above named as associated with the idea of faith, has the antagonism been removed, and thus is it still being re-

moved, and the opposition so disarmed, that
the finer, and purely spiritual manifestations
begin to be received by those who have
clambered over the stumbling-blocks in their
way, and to the spiritually-developed the
things of the spirit begin to be opened, and
by them spiritually discerned. But, oh!
through what struggles, what sufferings has
this knowledge of spiritual things been
attained. The utter repudiation of the
possibility of spirit expression and communion has led to public and private persecu-
tion worthy of other days. Men have
charged the folly, if not the crime, of
superstition upon all the early votaries of
modern Spiritualism ; and public opinion,
instead of the burning stake, has been, and
still is, the fiery ordeal to which the conscientious believer finds himself bound in bitter
agony, whilst nearest and dearest friends are
willing to add fuel to the fire, and blow the
flame, till the victim yields his faith, or
through spiritual power is raised triumphantly, like the martyrs of old, above all
consciousness of suffering.

By degrees the supremacy of pure intellectual knowledge and insight is giving way ;
and, having become willing to throw aside

their conceit of intellect, men are beginning to sit down humbly before true spiritual culture, and receive the inspirations from spirit life that have long been waiting to bless them, but they would not accept. Their intellectual development has liberated men from those idle fears and low conceptions which formerly led to witchcraft and its fearful persecutions; whilst the same condition of development has led, at the outset of the investigation of modern Spiritualism, to purely intellectual conceptions of the subject, through inquiries originating in the head, much oftener than in the heart. The idle curiosity, flattering itself often under the guise of scientific authority, which has from the beginning put the questions suggested by its vain conceit, has been met and answered in a way well calculated to put it to the blush. The spirit of the inquiry has been promptly met by its brother spirit in the spirit life; and all by the force of laws which the wise in the wisdom of this earth have been slow to comprehend, assuming that they were already well enough informed on all matters of spirit life, power, and manifestation, because they had reached to a comprehension of some of the laws by which its Creator regulates his material creation.

It may be claimed by different branches of the Christian church, that they do not deny the proper supremacy of pure heart culture when brought into comparison with the wisdom of the head, though they perhaps have not distinctly recognized the antagonism which we have shown to exist. In the Catholic Church, particularly, has the position been maintained, and practically carried out, that the danger in giving free scope to intellectual investigation in spiritual things certainly, and perhaps to some extent in temporal things, was so great, that the popular mind could not bear exposure to it, and hence the argument in support of blind church rule, and mysterious rites in their religious services, conducted in an unknown tongue by the initiated priest. So, too, with the dogmas of the Protestant churches, insisted upon as articles of faith, and involving points of doctrine which had been worked out by the leaders of the Church, who alone could be lifted up to a true contemplation of their inner sense ; a position of strange inconsistency for Protestantism, as recognized by all freethinkers, and justly rebuked by the parent church. But, passing by this question of inconsistency, and admitting the merit in this fear of intellectual supremacy, let us look a little at the character of the substitute offered in compensation for the loss of the intellectual investigation which has not been permitted. It is in this direction, as it seems to us, that the Church has deceived itself, and out of this self-deception that it is so powerless to put an end to the fearful sway of selfishness, which now rules with nations and individuals. So much stress has been laid upon the importance of articles of faith, that the masses have been content with holding to these, if indeed they have not been directly taught that these alone were sufficient for their salvation. Catholicism and dogmatic Protestantism have pointed out a danger in too independent action of the intellect upon spiritual things, but their position in this regard has been substantially a negative one only, so long as they have furnished no better substitute for the right of free inquiry than simple obedience to their own authority, whether expressed in blind church rule, or theological dogmas. Thus has it happened that all the while, in spite of Catholic church rule and Protestant dogmatic authority, the intellectual forces of men, starved into independent self-reliant action, have been attaining the ascendancy each day more and more, and the antagonism of which we have spoken become established.

If the Church had not assumed to possess all knowledge and all power in spiritual things, and taken upon itself the responsibility of true enlightenment, thus relieving men of their individual responsibility to know and understand their true relation to God and their fellow-men ; if it had not offered itself as the Mediator between them and their Creator, but had rather denied itself alway, and offered Christ as the only Mediator ; if by its own example it had taught men to humble themselves, each one, before God, in prayer for such light and such blessings as he might see were needed, and vouchsafe to send them ; then indeed would a good work have been done, and the Church of this day been entitled to a tribute of praise and thanks from its equally humble followers. But pride, conceit, and self-reliance have been its attributes, and its children could hardly be expected to be superior to their spiritual guide. The happy middle course of humble, prayerful, individual development was hard to find out under such conditions; and few, very few, have found and followed it.

We do not understand, and would not for a moment suggest, that the intellectual faculties of our nature are to be lost, or even kept in abeyance, but made subordinate to pure heart or spiritual culture, so that only true knowledge can, and shall, be offered to man's comprehension. Then all things of the spirit shall be accepted by, and made reasonable to, the mental faculties, which will sit humbly waiting for God's movement, and not trusting in themselves to work out their own knowledge in their own way, which leadeth to destruction. The equal development of heart and head, the beautiful harmonious result of a true relation between the spiritual and mental forces, in which alone can be found the perfect man, is yet to come ; and the grave question now proposed to the world is, whether the time for the establishment of that harmonious relation is not at hand ! It can come in no other way than through a pure spiritual Christianity, such as the world has not seen yet, with the Christ spirit, and not human intellect, under any guise of creed or doctrine, recognized as the only test of a true church. It is then, and not till then, that the prayer so often on the lips of men is to be answered; then, when God's kingdom shall come, and his will be done on earth, even as it is done in heaven.

If it be true—and Spiritualists know it to be true—that messages from angel forerunners have announced the coming of that kingdom as close at hand, when Christ shall return to earth, and reign in the name of the Father, is it well, nay, is it safe, to pass the messengers, or the message, by unheeded? If it should be that they are messengers of truth, are you ready, are you prepared, to bear the *quickening power* of the Spirit? Already is it at the nation's door. Already have the elements of war and fratricidal strife in this people been worked out into fearful expression. Be not deceived because this appears to have been done by natural causes. Wait not till the influence has penetrated to the very hearthstones of your homes, for there too shall its quickening power yet be felt, and the elements of disease and death be driven out into expression more fearful even than on the battle-field. Purify your homes, purify your hearts, purify your bodies, purify your lives! Wait not for the purification which shall be a consuming fire. Even now does the mighty voice sound through the air, as heard of old by the Prophet of Revelations, and audible to him that hath an ear to hear are those momentous words, " BEHOLD, I MAKE ALL THINGS NEW !"

July, 1862.

ARTICLE III.

SPIRITUALISM AND MATERIAL INTERESTS.

Knowledge the foundation of a living Faith.— Spiritualism breaks up too absorbing devotion to material interests, and opens the way to nearer approach and indwelling of the very Highest.— The signs wanting which should "follow them that believe." — Our civil war and its lessons.— Of what avail this modern necromancy.— A new Dispensation?— Two exemplifications of the work of Modern Spiritualism, External and Internal.

"And he shewed me a pure river of water of life."

AGAIN we find ourselves filled to overflowing with thoughts restlessly demanding expression. Again we are moved by a deep heart-felt desire to communicate to others, would it could be to all the world, some idea of the rich blessing, the joy unspeakable, which we have received from a knowledge of things spiritual, as opened to us through Modern Spiritualism. We say *knowledge* of

things spiritual: for it is no conventional
creed; no philosophical, or mystical, shaping
of our human conceit; no ingenuity of our
poor brains. It is knowledge in very truth:
a certainty; an experience; a living reality;
without which now, life would become to us
almost insupportable, the world would seem
a barren waste deprived of the indispensable
sunlight of God's love. The soul recog-
nizes and rejoices over this blessing, the richest in the Father's bestowal, at all times, and
in all events. It is drawn in with every
breath; it courses through every vein; it
moves, it leads, it guides, it guards, in every
emotion, every thought, every action of our
waking, or sleeping existence. It is the
presence of the living God! The willing
spirit listens to its heart promptings, and
child like yields every wish of its own to the
gentle ruling of a Father's love. Under its
influence, human pride is let down from all
assumption and conceit. The soul recog-
nizes in its inner sense, and its outer experience, that the divine guidance is ever directing and helping in matters seemingly the
most trivial, as well as in those otherwise
supposed to be most momentous, and so goes
on in its daily occupation, rejoicing equally in

large and small duties, for in all and each, it
humbly feels that it is doing, or at least trying to do, only the Father's will.

As we look into the world of life around
us, we feel, we know, that there too, as well
as in ourselves, the power of God, is alive
and at work ; and no living creature, no created thing, is too insignificant to be a sharer
of our sympathy as coming from the hand of
the same maker with ourselves, and sustained
by the same love.   Thus no difference of external position, or surroundings ; no apparent preference or exaltation of one creature
above another, of one human being over his
fellows astonishes or deludes us into anything like creature worship, or brings any the
least desire to sacrifice to worldly pomp or
circumstance.   All creatures and all things
are in their proper sphere and place, moving
on in accordance with a mighty law of development, which no man can fully comprehend.
Happy those who can recognize the Father's
guiding and sustaining hand through it all.
Thrice happy those who can fall gently in
with the current, and acquiescing in the wisdom of all things, without struggle or resist-
ance, humbly seek the more to know and feel
the Father's ever present protection and

care, the more the course of events, near and
far, large and small, becomes complicated
and inexplicable to their feeble comprehension. Oh, that this faith, this living faith
could be a reality of experience to all. May
God's blessing go with our humble effort to
communicate and explain to others something of this life divine, so that the desire in
their hearts may unfold into a faith that shall
open them to the influences of the Holy
Spirit. Thou knowest, Father, that this
wish is expressed in no vain conceit of our
own wealth; that it is no foolish boast of the
blessings with which Thou hast crowned
our life. As we are true unto the truth as
it is in Christ, be Thou unto us, and unto
this labor!

"That the desire in their hearts may unfold into a faith that shall open them to the
influences of the Holy Spirit"! Let no
one take offence at this; but rather let every
one inquire soberly what it signifies. What
does it mean, that in this day of Christian
development, with so many men and women
to be found throughout this religiously enlightened people, who have experienced the
movings of the spirit within, and become, in
the church sense, reconciled unto God, and

with so many more who have felt their inner
natures touched by the divine presence, and
the secret chambers of their hearts illumined
by a divine light, not their own; what does
this call mean, which says to such, and we
gladly admit there are many such, that their
faith needs yet to be unfolded, and their
hearts to be "opened to the influences of the
Holy Spirit"? Certainly it is not intended
to be a captious, fault-finding complaint, or
rebuke. It is rather an invitation to still
further development, to a finer growth, a
higher life of the spirit, a more complete
realization, in every day practical life, of all
the blessings which are involved in, and
spring from, the Christian faith; a more
abundant blossoming and fruition in those
gifts and graces of the spirit, which in the
days of the early disciples of Jesus were distinctly recognized as the natural outgrowth,
as they were the visible evidences of a true
Christian life. The highest received Christianity of the churches of to-day, stops far
short in its practical outworking of the Christianity taught, and if we may believe the
record, actually realized amongst the early
converts, the first disciples of the humble
Nazarene. And this without any reason,

or explanation, offered or received ; and when
referred to by some honest inquirer for a
cause, is admitted, with the cold, insufficient
comment, that those times are not these
times. In other words, the men and women
of those days, when the world was almost
two thousand years younger in its development than now, are admitted to have been
capable of spiritual attainments, which we of
this day cannot aspire to ! What has the
world been about all this time, that such
should be the comparative condition of those
who are so apt, in all other things, to boast
of their modern civilization ? Can it be believed, that the good seed sown by the Master's hand has been all this time germinating,
the divine influence by him implanted upon
our earth sphere has been so long, and so
widely, rooting, without some progress in the
capacity of man's nature to receive, and express, a higher type of Christian development, than it was possible for the men of the
early centuries to attain ; instead of our being
unable even to equal them ! The truth is,
not only that the good seed has been germinating, but that the natural man has been
going through a process of decay. There
has been a breaking down of the walls of

the flesh ; human nature has been changing ;
becoming less and less gross in its animal development, and consequently more and more
susceptible to spirit influences ; and that the
manifestations of spirit presence and power
in these days, are uncontrovertible evidences
of the fact.   But we may be content, for the
present, to rise to those spiritual attainments
with which, the record tells us, the early
Christian disciples were blessed.   When
those are reached, it will be time enough to
aim at higher growth, and loftier elevations,
of the spirit's life.

The first step towards progress is the
admission of present wants, the acknowl-
edgment of present short comings, the
recognition of something better and higher,
which we have not yet reached.   Every one
admits that there is no condition so fatal to
Christian development, as a satisfaction and
contentment with present attainments.   In
order therefore that the class of professing
Christians, to whom we have above referred,
may be reminded how far short they are of
the living faith which Jesus offered to his
contemporaries, and by the wonderfully pre-
served record, as well as by the influences
now pouring in upon the world, offers unto

us, we would ask such to put a few searching questions to themselves, which shall reach to the heart, without disguise of any sort. When these questions have been seriously considered, they will be more willing to admit the necessity, and better able to receive the blessings, of a new dispensation, whose first work is to revivify the ancient faith which bears such stinted fruit in their lives.

Beginning with the more visible signs of faith ; where do we find a professor of the Christian life in these days who, through his religious development, can show, we do not say boast of, for they are in no sense a subject for pride, any of those signs, which in the words of Jesus, as recorded by St. Mark, " shall follow them that believe "—" In my name," said the Master, " shall they cast out devils ; they shall speak with new tongues ; they shall take up serpents ; and if they drink any deadly thing, it shall not hurt them ; they shall lay hands on the sick, and they shall recover " ! Who of them, we ask, can show a faith responsive to those other words recorded by St. John, " He that believeth on me, the works that I do, shall he do also, and greater works than these shall he do " ! Who, again we ask, can show any

of those gifts of the spirit enumerated by St.
Paul as the natural result and evidence of a
knowledge of Christ, when accompanied with
the gift of charity? How is it that none of
these persons can show even the signs and
gifts which have, in these latter days, made
their appearance amongst so many that are
not recognized as the truest followers of
Christ, if indeed they are not often wholly
without that spirit of charity, or love, the
want of which, says St. Paul so truly, renders
these gifts valueless. It may almost be said,
that instead of the members of the modern
Christian church showing in themselves any
of the gifts of the spirit, they are apt to condemn unheard any one who seems to possess
these gifts, as on that very account, to be
excluded from the Christian fold!

But passing by these external evidences
recognized by Christ himself as signs of
those who believe in him, what are the inner
proofs of progress in true Christian development to be found in the professing members
of the modern church? For example, how
many of these have comprehended the meaning, and practical application, of the Saviour's
reference to the lily of the field, as a beautiful exemplar for man to copy in his daily

life? How many are there who begin to take no thought for the morrow, what they shall eat, or what they shall drink, or wherewithal they shall be clothed? How many who really believe, and carry into practice their faith, that if they will seek the Kingdom of Heaven first, all those things "shall be added unto them." To earn a livelihood, to gain an independence, is proclaimed and approved as the great aim, the first object of every man's ambition; not to find out what service his Creator would have him do, what field is open for him to accomplish the highest, greatest good; not what the unselfish promptings of the spirit within would have him attain to, but what avenue is most open by which he can reach what his friends, and all the world, call success. Occasionally, to be sure, a young man begins his career with vague notions of usefulness; but they are either soon crushed out of him by contact with the stern realities of life, which come to try him, and prevail against his better feelings, for the reason that he has not that living faith which can sense and follow the leadings of the Spirit, and patiently leave results to the wisdom of God; or he sinks in despair at the apparent fruitlessness of his efforts, and dies early of a broken heart. The pulpit does indeed insist upon the absolute importance of every man's loving God with his whole heart, being just in all his dealings, and in short carrying his religion into his business; but does it sufficiently teach that a true development in Christ is itself a business, the first business, it may almost be said, the only business that peremptorily demands his attention; for the Kingdom of Heaven first attained, the fruits of all other business shall, in natural course, be added unto, and crown his life with many joys. Men and women have yet to feel that in the performance of all the daily avocations of life, in every position and capacity, they are doing God's business, not their own! When they can feel this, the work of life, in all its details, will go on with a harmony that shall chord with the very music of the spheres; for then will they have sought the Kingdom of Heaven first, and will do their daily labor, not for the sake of the bread that shall be earned by it, but for the joy in doing the Father's will; trusting that their daily bread will be given to them in due season in answer to their daily prayer, as naturally, and as surely, as the elements bring to the lily of the field the food it needs for its daily growth, and the materials wherewith to weave the beautiful fabric of its matchless raiment.

A much severer test of the development of those who openly and formally profess their faith in Christ, is to be found in their conduct at this period of national judgment[1] and condemnation, when if ever there seems to be a call for all the cardinal Christian virtues, FAITH, HOPE, and CHARITY. We feel that the leading spirit of the great Southern Rebellion is a wicked one. We believe equally, that many, if not the most of the combatants on both sides, certainly of those who have gone forth to crush it with death-bearing weapons of war, have been, and are, actuated by their highest sense of self-sacrificing duty, and shall receive their reward accordingly. But do these considerations alter the fact that war is not, and cannot by any sophistry be made, consistent with the teachings of the gentle Jesus, whom they in other things profess to follow. Undoubtedly every man does right who acts up to his highest sense of duty ; but is that sense of duty necessarily according to the Christ-spirit of

[1] 1863.

love, because it is the man's highest sense? The highest sense of duty with the ancient Jew was in exact retaliation, "an eye for an eye, a tooth for a tooth." But Christ has taught, nay, in love commanded, "That ye resist not evil: but whosoever shall smite thee on thy right cheek, turn to him the other also." "Love your enemies, bless them that curse you, do good to them that hate you, and pray for them which despitefully use you and persecute you" are the words of the Master, spoken without reservation of any kind. Some persons, a little more tender than others, feeling the inconsistency, have talked about laying aside their Christianity for the war, as they, with their short external vision, have found themselves unable to see how the struggles of the day could be carried out to a successful issue without the recourse to arms; instead of acting up to their inner sense of Christian duty, and leaving results to Him who rejoices more to be worshipped as a God of love and peace, than appealed to as a God of battles. Have these persons forgotten how the walls of Jericho fell down at the sound of trumpets blown with a blast of *living faith!* Have they never read how, more than once, the

enemies of Israel were scattered by the inter-
position of divine power, without a blow
struck by the Sword of Gideon; and this
long before the people were blessed with the
light of the Gospels! Is it not time the
world began to understand, that if in the orderings of God's providence there is need of
men to fight, it is because there are men
whose progress in Christian development has
not yet rooted out the elements of war from
their natures. No pure health can be enjoyed by the human system so long as disease is lurking in the vital parts; and as long
as the passions that culminate in war are cir-
culating in humanity, no matter how deep
under the surface, so long will occasions be
presented for working them out; it being
always the prerogative of God, and of Him
only, to bring good out of this direful evil.

If we are asked what we would have men
do in this emergency of the nation's existence,
we would say, let every one go to his God in
humble, earnest prayer for such knowledge
as shall show him his highest duty, and when
found, do it unselfishly, with all his might.
Let him not however deceive himself by sup-
posing that he is therefore acting up to the
Christ teachings, because he is fulfilling what

he finds to be his highest duty. But let him rather pray the more earnestly to God that he may receive the true Christ spirit, and sense of Christian duty, the more he finds himself called to act at variance with the clear, unmistakable precepts of the Founder of his professed faith; for *it is a thing of growth*, and nothing short of miraculous intervention will give him the true sense, the true light at once. The trouble is, that men, having no knowledge of, and giving no recogni·ion to the guidance of the Spirit, use their minds first to find out what course of conduct to pursue, and then go to God to ask his help in carrying out *their* plans of management; instead of lifting up their hearts first in humble prayer to Him for guidance, and then following the lead of the Spirit with all their minds! Thus it is that we have had all the while the strange spectacle presented, apparently so contradictory, in the civil war now raging, of clergy and laity on both sides, sending up fervent appeals to their God of battles to bless each their cause, which each had previously in the exercise of their wise self-relying heads, stimulated more or less by their passions, determined should be maintained and defended by all the arts of war of which *modern Christian civilization* can boast!

In another relation, one which concerns humanity perhaps more nearly than any other, inasmuch as every child that is born into earth life is fashioned according to its conditions, we mean the marriage relation, we would ask, how nearly do men and women conform to the true Christ life? Is this relation conducted in accordance with that Christ spirit which teaches them to love one another as little children; and do they herein show forth a living faith in those words of Jesus, " Whom God hath joined, let no man put asunder"? The growing tendency in all legislation to facilitate divorce, is a short answer to the latter question; whilst the former is pointedly met, by simply referring to the little improvement in the human race, both in its physical and spiritual development, from generation to generation, notwithstanding its changing conditions. But we have too much to say upon this sacred topic, to enlarge upon it at this time.

Other points of view might be taken, from which a close scrutiny would show still further inconsistencies between the teachings of the Master, and the lives of his professed

followers.　Too long have these inconsistencies been allowed to remain unmolested ;
too often have they given opportunity to un-
believing critics to frame arguments against
Christianity, which no honest man can answer, and no sensitive soul hear without a
blush of shame.　They have been kept too
much out of sight, and considered too much
out of the reach of modern faith to remedy.
But we hasten to meet the inquiry, which we
feel is pressing upon us, " What has Modern
Spiritualism to offer towards helping men
out of these admitted inconsistencies?"　We
have been told, says the inquirer, from the
Master's own lips, that the hardness of heart,
which could not be touched by the sayings
of Moses and the Prophets, would "not believe, though one rose from the dead" ; and
it can hardly be supposed that any less efficacy to convert sinners is to be found in the
teachings of Jesus, than in the sayings of
Moses and the Prophets.　"Of what avail
to Christians then, this modern necromancy"!
　　An inquiry based upon such a suggestion
of argument, and it is the first suggested,
the most natural, and the most potent argument that can be used, indicates the idea of
Modern Spiritualism entertained by most

unbelievers, and indeed by many believers, that the whole meaning and value of the phenomena is, in establishing the fact, that the spirits of the departed do exist in spheres more or less near to the earth life, and in the accompanying joy of communing directly with them. The truth however is, and we would proclaim it to the ends of the earth, to the many Spiritualists who are yet groping about in search for it, and to the unbelievers who stand outside hardly condescending to recognize the simplest facts of the phenomena, much less trying to ascertain their meaning, the truth is, and herein lies the answer to the inquiry so directly put, that these new conditions, and apparently strange relations between the spirit and earth life, are chiefly important as means to a great end, namely *the more complete opening of the heart of humanity to the influences of the Holy Spirit!* Thus, whilst we admit that the mere raising of the spirits of the dead is not itself of vital importance, however novel and interesting, and does not of itself possess any power to save, we say that the influences which the spirits of the departed, coming with the angels of God, are now empowered to bring and communicate to those in the earth life, constitute a new element of power not before manifested or exercised, at least in the manner, and to the extent, now permitted in this the fulness of time. The value of Modern Spiritualism is not to be found in those physical manifestations which strike so many minds as too trivial to be worthy of the higher spirit life, nor in those communications, which, though often full of beauty and wisdom, do not inculcate any new doctrines of life, or in their highest reaches suggest any better teachings than those already handed down to this generation in the blessed words of Jesus. No, it is the influence of the Holy Spirit, which filled the souls of the early Apostles, and is now waiting to be poured into our hearts through this channel of communication, this instrumentality of God's appointment, that constitutes the real value, the momentous power and importance of Modern Spiritualism. That these things do not originate with man, most persons are now ready to admit. They are indeed of and from God. Christ cometh that all things may be fulfilled. Refuse not to believe because the manner of his coming is not in accordance with your expectations, or your human judgment of probabilities. Remember how the Jews stumbled, because they could not find in the humble Nazarene, those evidences of an earthly kingdom which they had anticipated. Like a thief in the night, is he coming; yet like a Prince of Peace. Oh blessed light that shines through the dark cloud which now hangs over this people, with a deepening gloom, unfathomable to the eye of reason. To the eye of faith, the living faith as it is in Christ, which can be known only through the heart, the silver lining of the dark shroud is visible, and a divine hope awakened to give new courage to suffering souls, which shall sustain them to the end.

Modern Spiritualism is then no new " Cultus," but rather a process in the development of an old " Cultus," amounting in its fullness to a new Dispensation. The spirit world, with all its quickening influences for good and for evil, is brought close to the earth life. The evil influences come to tempt, to try, to judge, and to be judged; ministering spirits and angels come also, not in idle pastime, but in serious, earnest endeavor to reach the hearts of those, who by inheritance, and their own contact with the exterior world, are hardened against the things of the spirit; and the labor has been, and is, to lift humanity into a condition receptive to the blessed influences which they have brought with them, even the influences of the Holy Spirit. Thus are all men to be raised up to a higher plane of spiritual vision, so that they can see and comprehend the meaning of the Scriptures, which are illuminated by this increased light. The truths in the teachings of Jesus are now vitalizing to the conception of believers. There is no longer occasion for scholastic criticism, or learned intellectual disputations, on the meanings of words; for the meaning intended to be conveyed by them, their true spiritual power and influence, flows out into the receptive soul independently of the mere dress, the external form of its expression. As in the days of their utterance, the words of Jesus were heard, but not understood; so in this latter day, their deep meaning, their full significance, their hidden power, their life-giving influence has not reached the individual hearts of the people, or never could the inconsistencies, and short-comings, be found in the modern Christian life to which we have referred. It is by opening the hearts of the men and women of this generation, so that having ears to hear, they may hear and comprehend, and carry out into practice, those very teachings of Jesus, that the revival of the ancient faith, the first great work of this new dispensation, is to be accomplished. Already has this work been begun with thousands of quiet Spiritualists, who are patiently waiting on the Lord ; whilst the ever active and forth putting influences of Anti-Christ have endeavored to fasten upon the cause, the stigma of Bible Infidelity.

The power of this spirit influence is beginning to be made manifest in the development of knowledge of things spiritual, which is yet to be a wonder to the world. Only the germs of truth lie, more or less concealed, in the brief recorded teachings of Jesus. Germs of all truth they are, and first planted upon the earth sphere by him, through the grace of God, more than eighteen centuries ago. They have been all this while working their way through the crust of earth, their delicate points cleaving the hard-hearted soil in which they were set, and now, touched by the quickening rays of the returning Sun of righteousness, are beginning to send their branches out, and to spring forth to a growth, that shall be worthy of the long preparation.

We are lost in contemplation of the possibilities of development in man's nature and surroundings, through his spiritual progression.
These are, and will be, the natural growth of
seeds already sown. They cannot pretend
to be of any other, or higher origin than the
early Christ germs; but in their development, there should be expected, in all phases
of being, really new manifestations, new
thoughts, a new understanding of the various works of creation, new conceptions of
the earth life and its relations to the spirit
world, which, as they spring forth, will ar-
range themselves, like new leaves in beautiful order, on the broad and ever spreading
tree of knowledge.

We should be glad to explain our meaning more at length, but must content ourselves, for the present, with a brief reference
to two exemplifications, from among the
many which have come within our experience. The first of these, we find in a very
beautiful and interesting manifestation of
spirit presence and power, recently given in
our presence, through a Medium, whose
own spiritual condition is a sad evidence,
amongst the many we have known, that
physical manifestations have in themselves

no saving grace, no healing power, but are only the necessary means of breaking down the obstacles which in this day of materialism, prevent the access, and impede the growth, of a living faith. After several other experimental tests, not particularly interesting to us, though calculated to astonish, and at least puzzle, a fresh inquirer into the phenomena; a piece of plain white card board, which had been carefully marked so as to identify it, was placed in the left hand of one of the company who sat next to the Medium. In the right hand of the same person were placed three pencils, two of crayon, colored red and green, and one of common black lead, so that they extended horizontally over the card board, and about two inches above it. The card board and pencils, in the position described were then held by the same person under the table, out of sight; whilst the hands of all the others present were placed upon the table. Within half a minute, the card board was produced, and to the astonishment and delight of all, there appeared upon its before unsullied surface a beautiful wreath, delicately drawn and colored, the vine and leaves in green, thick set with red roses in bud and full bloom, and within the wreath, finely written in black lead, but distinctly legible, a message of love signed by the name of a child, who was in the spirit world, unbeknown to the Medium, and to most of those present. Upon inquiry, it appeared, that the pencils had remained during their concealment, in the same position as first placed, a slight vibration in them only having been recognized. Our theory of the process was, that the picture was first conceived complete in its spirit form, then brought near to the card board and pencils, so that the elements of color could be abstracted from the pencils, and, as it were, photographed upon the card board by a power, of which we as yet know nothing beyond this suggestion of its existence. We could not resist the further reflection that in time to come, it may be long years yet, the relations of humanity to the spirit world might be so far changed and advanced, that this power could be brought into common practical use, in a way that would lift art to a pinnacle of power and beauty never before dreamed of.

Our other exemplification is not an external manifestation, but an internal unfolding. Through Modern Spiritualism we have arrived at an understanding of the origin,

growth, and purpose of all earth life, of which
we before had no conception. This understanding, like all our knowledge of things
spiritual, apart from their phenomenal manifestations, is a natural out-growth in our
minds, stimulated into life by the influences
with which we were first brought into communion through the person, to whose deep
religious nature, and spiritual development,
we have before referred. Little by little,
sometimes quite disconnectedly, with occasional direct promptings, have these thoughts
come to us, and by slow degrees gathered to
make a symmetrical, harmonious philosophy
of nature, which we feel is very truth, for it
is from God. Perhaps some of the ideas,
possibly all of them, for we are yet in our
childhood, just beginning to read the book
of life, have been given to the world in days
gone by; but they come to us anew as inspiration, for which we thank only the Giver
of all good gifts. Every growing thing on
the earth plane has its spirit life and form,
and is but the external expression of the spirit reality, the earthly habiliment of spirit life,
made thus external, in order to be cognizable to humanity. Let us confine our observation to one phase of this external expression;

for instance, to vegetable life. We find then
that the office of the earth-born flower is,
not merely to delight the senses of man, and
amuse his hours of idleness or recreation, but
more than all, to throw upon him influences
directly from the spirit life, of which it is the
medium of expression to his earthly sense.
In form and color suggestive of harmony,
they accomplish much; but as mediums for
the transmission, sometimes of a life-giving
fragrance, and sometimes of a noxious poison,
do the flowers of earth now appear to us as
acting a most important part in the development of humanity. The odor is itself of
spirit origin, and exists in spirit life, the
flower being the naturally appointed agent,
or medium, to express it on the earth plane.
Herein we find an explanation of what has
heretofore been an inexplicable mystery to
the best of science, namely, how the fragrance
could be continually given forth, a real essence filling the air, and yet no discoverable
reduction, or abstraction, of the substance of
the flower. The skilful anatomist has dis-
sected these little creatures of God's love
down into their most inmost recesses, where
the odor seems to have its birth-place; but
the mystery is still unsolved, until we con-

ceive the idea of fragrance existing first in the spirit life, and then poured through these delicate organisms of divine appointment, and made cognizable to human sense. The flower in fact gives nothing forth from itself, but is only the conduit, the beautiful medium for external expression of spirit life and power, and is able, be it never so tender and delicate, to continue its functions of transmission, whilst its natural life is prolonged.

Let us carry this conception a little further. Does it not throw a flood of light upon the mystery of human life? What are human beings, but the external expressions, upon the earth plane, of spirit forms and spirit life. What are we but mediums, all and each, in varying degrees, for the outward manifestation of good and evil influences, that are thrown into, and poured through us, for the world's weal or woe? In one respect we differ from the flower, and that is in the capability of our natures in great measure to determine for ourselves, under the grace of God, whether we will continue to be channels for the communication of much evil, mingled with a little good, or whether we will become so purified, through the life that is in Christ, that none but pure influences shall be made manifest in our lives. The subject is capable of indefinite extension. We leave it here, with the earnest prayer that all men may soon accept its deep significance, and ever remember, that it lies with each one to determine, whether he will draw from his surroundings, and give forth in his life, poisonous elements of evil ; or whether he will spread far and wide only such sweet, life-giving fragrance as the Father's love vouchsafes to dispense through him unto his race.

But interesting, as we must admit such trains of thought have been, and are to our minds, they are like all philosophizing, insufficient food to satisfy those yearnings of the spirit which reach up after the Father's love, as its only true life. To drink from that fountain, " whose water shall be in those who drink it, a well of water springing up unto everlasting life," this should be the longing, as it is the greatest joy of the soul. We welcome then those influences which will aid, as they have already aided many, in finding that fountain of living waters, by opening the heart and mind to a true reception and understanding of the teachings of Jesus. And especially would we remember, and try

to comprehend the deep import of, that saying of the Master, " He that rejecteth me
and receiveth not my words, hath one that
judgeth him, the Word that I have spoken,
the same shall judge him on the last day."
We feel, we know, that these words have a
significant application to this day and hour.
Christ, the Master, calls us to look into ourselves, and out of our own mouths to save
or to condemn.   The Bridegroom cometh,
we know not the day, nor the hour; but he
cometh, and the angels are preparing the way.
The evil that is in men must be eradicated,
burned out from the face of the earth; and
it will be done, nay is doing now; the elements are now gathering in for the final day,
when God, through Christ, shall reign.   As
the lightning shineth from the East unto the
West so is the Christ influence now spreading, and spread, over the earth, quickening
every good and evil element of life into new
and unwonted activity.   It is idle to attempt
to fix any period according to our finite
measure of time, when the culmination of
these passing events shall be brought about.
It may be many years yet : the processes of
God's providence have ever been gradual in
their development.   We know not the day

nor the hour. We know, we can know, only the duties which each day and hour, as they come, bring with them; and this is enough, for it demands all our best energies to fulfil these duties with our whole heart. Under the Father's blessing, influences from the spirit world have now come to help us in their daily fulfilment, so that through a knowledge of God, we can say in very truth, in every moment of each day, that we are doing His will; that His business is our business, and our business His; that our great desire is to be humbly worthy to receive the blessed salutation from the Master, "well done good and faithful servant." Thus, and thus only, will the selfish ends of life be lost sight of; thus will men labor at their daily avocations, not to earn the means to gratify their selfish desires, but to do God service. Thus will they be practically seeking first the Kingdom of Heaven; and as surely as there is a living God, shall all necessary things, whether in their spiritual or material wants, be added unto them.

Let us then, each and all, thank God for the new Dispensation, whose work is only commenced when men, through its influences, begin to understand truly, and to carry into practice, the teachings of the Holy Book. In other ways of its own is it bringing, and will it bring men to the fountain of life, from which it is itself an out-pouring, the sweet savor of whose waters shall entice all who drink of it to follow the *living* stream up to its *living* head. Behold !—that "pure RIVER of WATER of LIFE, clear as crystal, proceeding out of the throne of GOD, and of the LAMB. In the midst of the street of it, on either side of the river, *is* the TREE of LIFE : " * * * " And the leaves of the tree *are* for the healing of the NATIONS."

January, 1863.

THE PURITY AND DESTINY OF MODERN SPIRITUALISM.

Second Series.

"*All history shows that the first article of a saving faith, for any land or time, is faith that there is a Power in this universe strong enough to make truth-seeking safe, and good enough to make truth-telling useful.*"

PRES. A. D. WHITE,
Cornell.

SECOND SERIES.

1883.

To minds familiar with modern things of the spirit, which are rapidly ceasing to be the strange mysteries they at first appeared, though yet only partially opened, there may seem to be little that is new in these pages. But they have been written, and are now published, for the uninitiated, as well as for those acquainted with the facts and experiences. Through all there has been no seeking after novelty, but rather and only for the truth.

Should some of the inquiry seem like probing into the ways of God, or too much like that feeling after the " print of the nails," which alone could persuade the doubting disciple, the writer can only say that it is in accord with the need of his own mind, as well as with the development of the day, that man should in all things find a " reason for his faith," if he can ; the limit of such inquiry, though not always of his attainment, being only in his capacity to shape his questioning.   Not in conceit or presumption let the asking mind raise its thought to the highest, but in that sure trust which should ever bring the sincere child to the good Father, with uplifted head and outstretched arms, for the blessings of His great love, the inspiration of His ever waiting spirit of truth.

ARTICLE IV.

Spiritualism the Opening Way.

An emblem strangely found. — Various good shown.
— Gifts of the Spirit. — Efficacy of prayer. — Individual freedom. — No eternal punishment. —
Neglected opportunities. — No concealment of
wrong doing. — Freedom in love to be in service of God. — Supremacy of the Spiritual. —
Errors committed. — Forces of the new Dispensation. — Methods, meaning, and mission of spirit
workers. — Trials of Mediumship. — Appeal to
the churches.

"Unto the Jews a stumbling-block, and
unto the Greeks foolishness," were the
words written eighteen centuries ago, of the
dispensation then opening. History repeats
itself; and again the announcement of new
truth, and a greater possibility in the world's
development, has proved a stumbling-block
to many. To others, and these no longer
an exceptional few, Modern Spiritualism has
proved An Opening Way, — often through

struggle which has seemed like climbing the very steeps of Calvary, to be rewarded at the summit with such joyful assurance, such peaceful outlook, such knowledge, and such faith, as have well repaid all the toil and pain of the sharp ascent. Largely out of knowledge so attained and assured, these pages are written.

Walking one day of December, 1862, upon a familiar railroad causeway within the limits of Boston, our attention was drawn to a piece of granitic quartz, lying among the ten thousand other stones which formed the gravelly embankment. On picking it up and turning it over we found that a portion of the stone had crumbled out from the under side, so as to leave two veins of white quartz, easily recognized, though roughly broken, to be in the form of the Christian cross. We accepted the emblem with joy and trembling. Such, we thought, had been our experience in the cause of modern Spiritualism. Drawn first to examine the external phenomena seemingly from motives of curiosity, we had learned, upon entering deeper into the examination, that we had found no bauble with which to amuse an idle hour, but had taken up the cause, the very cross of Christ, — the cross, because it had been the occasion of the deepest suffering in our life hitherto; and of Christ, because the suffering had come ever out of our desire and persistent search after the true way of life in all things, both of the body and spirit.

Under similar promptings and convictions others have entered upon labors to which they have felt themselves called in the name of Spiritualism, through trial and suffering finding their better purification. Many inquirers, however, have been prone to think that in their simple acceptance of the spiritual phenomena they have not only found the way to heaven, but have entered the very gates! To such we would say, there is no high-road opened now, more than before, upon which an idler has merely to set his foot and find himself drawn up to the heavenly mansions without effort or labor on his part. The recorded errors of early Spiritualists are like gravestones, marking the spots where the seekers after modern spiritual things have been drawn off into pitfalls sunk of old to catch all who might wander from the true path; while the successes of others only point the way up the steep ascent, which is yet full of dangers and obstacles. That these difficulties should become less and less numerous, and more easily overcome as the pilgrim advances in the search after truth, is to be expected, and will be realized in proportion as he is faithful to his highest promptings at and from the start; and so each succeeding generation of men will advance on the pathway of true life, as the generation passing away has brought the race nearer to a condition able to welcome the coming of God's kingdom. But there is work, much work, to be done yet.

It may help the minds of those who are not likely to come otherwise into present contact with what seems to us a momentous subject, to learn something of the work it has accomplished and is still doing in the development of ideas essential to man's progress, against the continued indifference or opposition of the most cultured minds, and the united desire and effort of old science to put down the ghost that will keep rising, with ever-renewed power, to baffle and disappoint all efforts for its suppression. The old cry, " Who will show us any good ? " is repeated by many of Modern Spiritualism. Having found much good, we would endeavor to show it to others, — not for the sake of proselyting, for experience has shown too well that belief in these things cannot be forced before its time, but for the enlightenment of many who, having never sought to penetrate within even the outermost circle of physical manifestations, are waiting the good Father's time to bring them into the fold which we believe will some day hold all the children of men.

The most obvious good from the advent of Modern Spiritualism would seem to be the demonstration or evidence of things *heretofore unseen*, which is given in its simplest manifestations. Doubtless there are many minds so well settled — it may be only through inheritance and unquestioning habit — in their convictions as to the momentous question of the after-life, that it is not easy for them to understand the needs of the very many others who, in seeking a reason for the faith that was in them, have been led off into the wilds of mysticism, or lost in the desert sands of materialism, and to whom the lowest forms of modern spiritual manifestations have brought the only light that could help them out of their difficulties. The tiny raps, so much abused by the wise in the wisdom of

earth, have brought such comforting assurance
to minds desponding of the future state, as all
the reasoning of the pulpit and the demonstrations of mundane science could not have
begun to afford. More than one proud philosopher has come down upon his knees before
these simplest evidences of a continuing existence, and thanked the good Father that a way
had been at last opened to him, small though
it be, leading up to the heavenly mansions.
Admitting, for the argument, the uncertainties
of identity in spirit communication, the bare
fact of these little sounds being produced under the guidance of an intelligent power, and
coming plainly from behind that veil hitherto
so impenetrable, has reached the minds too
long habituated to material evidences to be
able to spiritually discern a spirit presence.
This age of material advancement could not,
at first, have recognized the nearer approach
of the spirit spheres, except through material
manifestations; and in time we believe the
age will lift its hands in gratitude for the
evidences, however humble, vouchsafed to its
great need !

As the next obvious good, may perhaps
be named the testimony of Modern Spiritualism upon the subject of Faith, which has

occupied the Christian mind so much. The saving faith insisted upon so strenuously by evangelical disputants, as a condition precedent to salvation, and made a requirement of the church-member without which there could be no fellowship, under the light of Spiritualism is shown to be only a compliance with the common law of all life ; *viz.*, that neither good nor evil can reach an unwilling recipient as they can the willing mind, and that nothing is so sure to impede progress in any direction as the lack of willingness to receive truth, whether it accord with preconceived opinions or not. Having once formulated its dogmas, the Church has been prone to resist innovation, and thereby necessarily to retard growth in any direction of thought not in harmony with its settled creeds. It has been slow to understand the simple meaning of such words of the Master as "Thy faith hath made thee whole,"— attributing a mystical value to the acceptation of certain forms of belief, when the whole virtue of the condition denominated Faith is simply in its receptivity, or willingness to receive. The testimony of Spiritualism in this direction is interesting and instructive, showing through all the forms

of manifestation the same undeviating law,
whether in the first approaches of opinionated
scientists to the simplest physical demonstrations of the after-life, or in the seekings
of avowed believers after the more hidden
things of the spirit, where the faculty of
spiritual discernment is called into action.
The state of mind of the investigator has
again and again proved a stumbling-block
to the manifestations, when the gathering
has been made wholly or mostly of scientific
experts, who will insist upon applying their
old mundane tape-measure to conditions utterly foreign to such use. Often, too, have
companies of avowed Spiritualists failed to
reach the inner sanctuary by their lack of
the childlike receptive condition of mind,
which alone can find out the heavenly mysteries. The lesson shown in the violent
conversion of the Apostle Paul still fails to
reach the minds of men learned in things
pertaining to the earth plane, so that as a
class they will not, perhaps cannot, receive
the new philosophy, until brought into it
by some prostrating experience, from which
they may rise wiser and better men. The
few marked exceptions only serve, as usual,
to prove the rule ; and, as in other steps of

the world's development, the new knowledge
has found favor with the humbler, before
gradually working up into the higher walks
of earth life. Again and again, truth must
need be cradled in a manger. Should it be
said that such kind of receptive faith opens
the way to evil as well as good, the reply is
frankly: Yes; such is the law of our being.
The willingness to receive must ever be
directed to that which is good. We cannot
escape this responsibility: it is inherent in
the conditions of free-will, which is the birthright of humanity, and out of which will
come the glory and the joy of man's final
redemption.

To the fear sometimes expressed, that
such knowledge of things spiritual would
take away all occasion for that exercise of
faith which trusts where it cannot see, so
commended by the churches, and often
blindly held to be one of the saving graces
of the Christian profession, we would say
that man need not be troubled lest he will
ever advance so far in finding out God,
that there will be nothing left for him on
which to exercise this spirit of trust. As in
mundane science, the further the student
penetrates, the wider appears the field of

discovery yet to be explored, so in things spiritual the most gifted seer reports of the fathomless beyond — the ever-opening, ever-receding mysteries of God.

Another good brought by modern Spiritualism is the light it has thrown upon the efficacy of Prayer. Hesitating to believe that the great Mind, by whom the universe has come into being and is hourly sustained, can be sufficiently concerned with the little things of individual experience to answer the calls of humanity, and accepting the idea of law in all the outworkings of the Divine Being, men have inclined more and more to doubt the efficacy of prayer. Unable to see the method of response, they have denied the possibility. Spiritualism solves the problem by showing the method. Prayers are the expression of the soul's desires. Earnestness and sincerity are the chief requisites for their potency. Now, just as a parent or friend hearing the prayer, or — what is equivalent — knowing the deep desire of a child, will labor to bring a response and satisfy the longing if it seem wise and good, so the friends about us, unseen by the natural eye, are near enough to hear our prayers, to know our deep desires, and equally to labor for their satisfaction. That they can and do thus influence events, — by acting upon the minds of others in the form, in whose power it is to bring about the answer to our prayers, as well as in other ways' of their own, — is proved beyond a doubt by the facts of Modern Spiritualism. To the question which at once comes to the inquirer, Shall we then address our prayers to the spirits and not to God? our reply is certainly, No. We should cripple the very power we would call to our aid by such asking. The mighty Spirit of God pervades the denizens of the spirit spheres, operating through them as part of its myriad agencies, as it does in its more apparent outworkings through external humanity. The reaching after that Spirit sets into action all the springs of being that are situated or conditioned so as to be moved by it; and the prayer, instead of being limited to one sole agency, as it would be if addressed to one known spirit in the spheres about us, may call to our aid many unseen and unknown influences, glad to be the instruments of the divine Mind in answering the cries of earth's children. The use of prayer as a means or condition for bringing the soul into harmony with God is

distinct from its efficacy for special response;
but, in this direction also, Spiritualism shows
how prayer to the good Father will move his
loving angels to bring the heavenly peace
and strength to the communing soul.

Another good in Spiritualism is its encouragement of Individuality, and independence
of the old bonds of Creed and Church. No
reliance on what another has done or suffered,
no passport from any church, no forgiving of
sins by the mouth of any prelate, no assumption of another's holiness, proves to be of
avail, according to the unvarying testimony of
Spiritualism.   Every man must work out his
own salvation : not without help from others,
it may be, — for we are all members one of
another,— but without benefit of the passion
of any other, save as it has operated to show
the way of life and instil the principle of
sacrifice.   To Liberal Christianity such views
are not new ; but the testimony of Spiritualism is not therefore to be repulsed : rather is
it to be welcomed as a coadjutor in the work
of liberalizing all churches ; for it is testimony, not argument — evidence, not asser-
tion.   Silently, but surely, it is doing its
work in this direction, as is apparent to every
unprejudiced observer; — co-operating with

and stimulating the efforts of the human
mind of this day and generation to an understanding, such as has not yet been attained,
of the "liberty wherewith Christ hath made
us free." "Spiritualism," says a recent inspirational speaker, "teaches the necessity of
good works done for humanity, rather than
intellectual submission to a tenet. The spirits
who claim happy states of life [in the spirit
spheres] invariably ascribe their condition
to deeds rather than creeds."

Interesting and important, too, is the testimony of Spiritualism upon the question of
an Eternal Hell, for so many years one of
the cherished tenets of the Christian Church
and still dwarfing by its terrors no small portion of the Christian fold. That there is
punishment, and enough of it, for all the
misdeeds of earth-life, is sadly proved by the
"cries of remorse from those in the shadowy
places" of the world beyond; but everywhere and under all conditions the law of
progression and development is proclaimed.
The eternity (*aion*) of punishment is not
everlasting, but, as the Greek word properly
translated means, it is of indefinite duration,
and determined by laws of being and states
of life of which we know as yet but little,—

pointing, however, always to a possible ter-
mination of the retribution, which has come
as the inevitable judgment of divine law
broken or unheeded in earth life. As the
kingdom of heaven was proclaimed to be
within, so are the judgment-seat and the
terrors of hell, according to Spiritualism,—
each having its natural and necessary outworking and manifestation in surroundings
which belong to the spiritual states so described. Dark as Erebus are the shadows
enveloping some unhappy spirits, as they are
seen by seers sufficiently developed; and
bright as the natural eye has never seen, are
the shining raiments of the "just made perfect."

In this connection may be stated the testimony from the spirit-spheres as to the suffering consequent upon neglect of opportunities
for good, as well as wrong done. Frequently
this is given in regard to the use of property
during earth-life, and in the final disposition
at its close. Holding with unrecognized
greed to the things of earth, the earth-bound
spirit, ere it passes beyond the control of its
material possessions, too often seeks to tie
the hands, and hearts too, of those who are
to come into possession, and by ingenious

devices to continue the sense of holding and
controlling what it knows it must soon sur-
render. When such a spirit has passed over
the river it cannot rise, because of the weight
of neglected opportunities. It comes back ;
nay, it has not left the earth, though out of
its material form, and cannot leave it, for the
heavenly spheres, until relieved in some way
of the terrible burden of misused earthly possessions. Fear of retribution is not the highest motive to appeal to ; love, not fear, should
be, and surely is to be, the rule of earth-life,
as well as of the heavenly spheres. But the
knowledge, — for it is knowledge, — which
comes from the unvarying testimony of
Spiritualism in this regard, must be a help to
some minds thus led to hesitate ; men otherwise unmoved would become accessible to
the approaches of their better angels, and
obedient to the promptings of their own
better natures.

Again, Spiritualism has done and is doing
good by demonstrating the folly of attempting to conceal wrong. Mankind instinct-
ively feel that the all-seeing Eye is upon
them ; but the universality of the fact, and
the seeming distance of the Ruler of the
universe, encourage wrong-doers to a strange

indifference to what should be a potently restraining influence. Shutting their eyes to God, they half believe that he is not looking at them when the moment of temptation and yielding comes. When it is understood that God sees and acts through many agencies, and that he is indeed ever beholding all his children of earth through the watchful eyes of dear ones " gone before," — that a " cloud of witnesses " is at our right hand and at our left, counting among its number a father or mother, sister or brother, the nearest, dearest friend perhaps we have known, — it must "give us pause," as it does and often has to sincere Spiritualists, when we are led into paths of danger. The angel bands can and do bring helping hands and new strength in the hour of our need. They can and do thus aid those who are unable yet to recognize or admit the possibility of their ministrations, — but under difficulty, because of the unbelief which repels their approaches and continually checks the good they would gladly do Witnesses they are of our daily acts and thoughts ; closer than we know they come into our lives and have access to our inner chambers. From them, as from God

and our own selves, there is no concealment.

From them, too, we learn the error of
the old saying, " Speak nothing but good
of the dead." They come to us from their
spirit abodes with their eyes opened to any
ill conditions in which they have been
removed from earth-life, and with entreaties
urge upon us to help them relieve their
souls of the weight of their wrong-doing by
confession of the most open kind. Speak
truth of the dead, is the new teaching; but
speak it kindly, tenderly, forgivingly. Having sought to cover up their wrong-doing
when in earth-life, they return to relieve the
burden of sin by acknowledging the wrong
and seeking forgiveness of the injured.
Again and again has this been demonstrated
to inquirers into Spiritualism. Again and
again has the cry come back from the
"spheres beyond," beseeching that there
should be no more concealment, but open
confession and endeavor to right the wrong.

More valuable to many minds has been
the development, through Spiritualism, of
the ancient gifts of the spirit, which had so
nearly died out. Of themselves deeply interesting and important, their recent man-

ifestation has illuminated the records of past
ages, especially of the early centuries of the
Christian Church, and helped many persons
to accept the testimony of those days who
could not before believe. In general it may
be said that Spiritualism has thrown a light
upon the Scriptures which was greatly
needed by this doubting, questioning, probing age; and with all the talk of some
extremists about throwing the Bible away,
it has brought to many, many inquirers
illustration and explanation of the old records which has given them new meaning
and value. We heartily commend the testimony of Spiritualism to all who need help
in this direction.

To our mind the work of modern Spiritualism upon social questions, and especially
upon the marriage relation, has seemed perhaps the most interesting and important.
While it is to be admitted that varying ideas
of the marriage relation have been expressed
through spirit mediums, and some on a low
plane of selfishness, we hold that on one
point the testimony of the spirit-spheres has
been uniform, — though with varying application, according to the development of the
communicating spirit, or of the medium, or

of the inquirer, or perhaps of them all.
This point is, freedom for the love principle manifested in the marriage relation.
That this freedom in its spiritual sense does
not mean wild license ; that it has regard to
the eternal principle of truth, and must ever
be held to that " service " of God " which
alone is perfect freedom," — there can be no
doubt. Its practical application to the marriage relation is a call for purity, — for freedom from the tyrannical power of lust, and
the abuse of opportunity under cover of
law. It asserts the right, the bounden duty,
rather, of woman, to whom the duty first
belongs, to protect the fountains of life from
every approach that is not actuated by love,
and to hold the marriage relation sacred to
the cause of parentage, for which it was
divinely instituted. The free love of pure
Spiritualism is, in fact, above the present
development of most men and women, and
not to be easily attained.

But this idea of freedom emanating from
the higher spirit-spheres, in its simple statement, is one thing ; in its form of acceptation and outworking it may be quite another,
and varies according to the conditions of
development it finds to work upon. Thus

it has come that so many phases of it
have been manifested through mediums and
among Spiritualists; some of which have so
justly offended the better sense of those
still abiding under the old dispensation.
How the freedom proclaimed for woman
has been misinterpreted,— how it has been
construed into a warrant for open breach
of the laws of the land, and bold defiance
of established usage, threatening sometimes
to subvert all social order, and causing the
very name of Spiritualism to be an offence,
— is too well known to be rehearsed here.
The fault has been not in Spiritualism, but
in its professors, who have fallen into error
out of their former states. Early Christianity had to pass through similar experience.
The sharp rebukes in some of the epistles to
the recently converted heathens of Corinth,
show plainly how they committed excesses
of intemperance, and yet graver offences, at
their love-feasts. They could not bear the
opportunity offered in the new rites, which
proved a temptation to their old conditions.
How mistaken the more sober-minded of
the unconverted of the Corinthians would
have been, to attribute to Christianity the
vices which seemed thus to find expression

through the Christian rites, we of this day
can easily see. Not less mistaken are those
who attribute to Spiritualism the excesses
of some of its believers, which are only
evidences of the low grade of development
they had attained under their old dispensation. Let not the uninitiated be too ready
to believe that such extravagances show the
real meaning of the doctrine, or illustrate the
low degree of the angel messengers who
brought it. Rather let them inquire into
the inner mystery of the opening dispensation of love, and learn how far it is above
the average development of our race to-day,
and to what heights of aspiration and attainment it is now calling the children of earth.

To the command, given of old, to subdue
the earth, no higher obedience can be ren-
dered by man than this subjection of the
appetites of the physical to his spiritual
nature. In other and less difficult ways
must he learn obedience before he can attain this greatest of his achievements. In
all the conditions of his natural life which
combine to make up his physical well-being,
especially in the food with which he builds
up and repairs the daily waste of his body,
must he learn to give heed to the voice

within, selecting ever that which will conduce to the welfare of both body and mind, — habit soon making easy and joyful what at first may seem like sacrifice.

There must be struggle to attain all this, taking man as he is in his best average development; and patience, too, — " patience with one another, patience with ourselves, patience with God," — ere the great end will be reached. That the millennial day is to come, is believed by most Christians. It is to be brought about, not by any cataclysm, not by any sudden fiat of the Almighty, but by and through better men and better women, better institutions, better philosophy, better teachings, better lives. Man can never reach his highest development until woman rises to the dignity of her great calling, and, holding herself obedient to the voice of the Spirit, brings herself and him into perfect accord with the Father's will in all these things.

These high doctrines in relation to the marriage state came to us in our contemplations many years ago, and were confirmed by the influences ready to communicate through the medium before referred to. Since then we have more than once reasoned upon the subject with communicating intelligences, and with mediums whose life-experiences had brought them to a recognition of the higher law. Thus, — while admitting that lower promptings, even to the lowest possible, have come from those in the spirit-world yet grovelling in the mire of their old earth-life, calling for the apostle's injunction, verily "to try the spirits," — we claim that these higher laws have been developed in the minds of truth-seekers in modern things of the spirit, and have been pronounced through their mediumship, by direct communication from their spirit-bands, and that such are now the accepted teachings among advanced spirits in the spheres above, as well as among those still in earth-life. Having studied the subject in its various aspects, and with ever earnest inquiry, since our first knowledge of these laws, we have found them in every way confirmed as rational and true.

We have thus spoken of some of the leading points in which Spiritualism is bringing its testimony and doing its work in aid of human development. A comprehensive view discloses the relation of this modern movement of the spirit-spheres to the dispensations which have preceded it, and especially its bearing upon the question of the Christ-coming, which is believed by so many Christians to be imminent at this time.

That it is ushering in a new dispensation, wherein spiritual power shall uproot the false developments of the day, break up the artificial systems — social, civil, and religious — by which man's higher nature is now fettered, and establish all the relations of life, all customs, institutions, and all philosophy, upon the firm basis of spiritual love and truth, is believed by most Spiritualists. Old creeds and dogmas wither before its fervent heat. Fermentation everywhere is trying the strength of old conditions, and bursting the bonds made up of falsehood and sham. But with all the seeming confusion there is underlying order, for the movement is sustained by the arm of the good Father, impelled and directed by his almighty will. It seems, indeed, the second Christ-coming; but not in the way expected by the Adventists, who, in their conception of a visible Messiah coming to judge the quick and the dead, are as mistaken as were the Jews of old in looking for a temporal kingdom under their expected leader. Did not the Christ-man say that he should come like a thief in the night?

Has he not come now, with his myriad angels, trying and judging from behind the clouds which screen the mighty presence from the material sight of earth-life? He comes, not as a personal king to erect a personal kingdom, but to establish the Christ-principle of divine love and truth in the minds and hearts of the children of men. God's kingdom is at hand, ushered in by the angels that know and do his will.

We understand the operation of spirit power in these latter days to be twofold. There is a widespread, general quickening of all the conditions of earth-life, affecting the good and the bad, the developed and the undeveloped, to activity beyond their usual state,—the Spirit of God moving over the deep; and there is a special, direct influence exercised by different spirits or bands of spirits upon individuals, according to the states in which they are found, — thus trying the condition of each and all, and quickening them to show their inner lives by deeds, and throw off, through sudden impulse often, the cloaks under which their real state has been concealed, perhaps even to themselves. In this way Spiritualism has sometimes seemed to encourage evil ways as well as good.

Closer observation shows that the law of individual responsibility is not to be broken.
The very possibility of low conditions in the
seeker after these things of the spirit opening
the way to and attracting undeveloped spirits,
who will be ready to encourage the low seeking, is only a call to every one now in earth-
form to look closely within, and see to it that
no evil conditions are lurking there, lest they
be quickened to expression beyond the control of their unhappy victim. The danger
is equally great, if not greater, because un-
perceived, though perhaps not so immediate,
if we do not directly seek communion with
the spirits; for they are about us, whether
we know it or not, watching every opportunity to reach and move us according to the
tendencies they find in us.

The movement of the spheres above has
come now because man has reached a point
in his development where he can and must
rise to better understanding and higher views
of the future, as well as of his present life.
To help that struggle for development,
Spiritualism suggests possibilities, not by way
of coercion, but of inducement for him to
come up higher. It is for him to receive the
suggestions, weigh them carefully in the bal-

ance of truth, by which he must test everything, and to reject or strive to live up to
them, according to his convictions. But let
him see to it that low motives do not underlie his own life, if he would distinguish the
true from the false. " Blessed are the pure
in heart, for they shall see God." Through
the wisdom of the pure heart, man must find
the truth of these latter days. " Try the
spirits," was the injunction given long ago.
It has momentous meaning now; but let us
remember that we, also, are being tried by
them, and see to it that our record will bear
their keen scrutiny. Judging and being
judged, they need our co-operation and help.
They call us to join with them in the great
work of redemption.

The words of a recent inspirational speaker
are apt in this connection : [1] " An impulsion
sweeps toward the earth ; every heart is
touched, every mind is delicately tried, every
soul is attuned ; those who are ready are at
once receptive. It is not simply that you
receive it when you seek, but you cannot
seek until there is some measure of truth
within you. It is not simply that it is forced
upon your brain and attention from the

[1] Mrs. Cora L. V. Richmond.

spiritual world, but you are tried and tested whether you are in any degree ready, or whether you are in any degree capable of serving the advancement of this thought; and the spirit-world know to whom they minister, — know to whom they bring the message of life; and it is brought to you according to your need."

To be true unto the truth, physically and spiritually, is the demand of the hour. He who fails in either will find out his weakness in the easy falling under temptation, and the lowering tone of his physical health, — happy if he is not brought into dire straits of bodily disease, or led out to be a monument of shame for his evil doings. It is more dangerous now for a man to come within the reach of temptation than it was thirty years ago, — there is such quickening of every element of his nature, causing the evil conditions to ferment and seek expression as never before.

Never was there a time in the world's history when there was so much need of the daily prayer, " Lead us not into temptation." The sunlight of God's love and truth is quickening all conditions with its kindling rays; and as the great deep bubbles and boils, impurities must need be brought to the surface, and at times seem almost to hopelessly cover and conceal the purer elements beneath. But love and truth will in the end prevail; God's kingdom will come, and humanity rise purified from the fiery trial.

Of Mediumship something should be said in this brief showing of the work, progress, and outlook of Modern Spiritualism. To those who have given the subject but little attention, mediumship is looked upon as a kind of cataleptic state, worthy of little consideration and less sympathy; the time having gone by when it was by the same persons deemed all trickery and deception. Closer observation shows that the world has never known greater occasion for kindly interest and helpful sympathy than is to be found in those who are called to the labor of aiding directly in the opening of this new dispensation through the intercommunion of the spirit-spheres and humanity in earth-life. All are one on both sides of the veil of time, — members one of another; the great family of man seems drawing together for such final occupation and enjoyment of earth and its attendant spheres as has been promised for the ransomed through all the centuries. The time is at hand for parting the veil which has heretofore screened the spirit-land from the vision of dwellers upon earth. The work to which mediums are called — to be channels of demonstration and communication, preparing the way for the more open intercourse yet to come — is of momentous value. That some, perhaps many, have not themselves understood the character of their calling, and so have failed to hold up the high standard of love and truth which would, at first thought, be expected of them, is to be attributed to the power of old conditions, out of which their spirits have not arisen; while yet they have been available for some phases of the work to be accomplished. Much may be said in extenuation of the shortcomings of mediumship. That it is no light calling, has been too often proved in the labors and sufferings of its subjects. It has been, indeed, a heavy cross to bear; not, however, without its crown, for it brings ever an underlying sense of happiness through all the suffering, with periods of exaltation hardly known without it. But none can know, who have not had the experience, what agony of spirit, and

sometimes acute physical pain, have been
borne by persons of mediumistic development in their contact with and rough usage
by conditions of earth-life wholly inapprecia-
tive of their delicate organization and sensitive state. " Father, forgive them, for they
know not what they do," has been wrung
from the lips of many a martyr since they
were first uttered by the great Sufferer ; but
never more than in these days of modern
mediumship. Surely these things ought to
be and will be soon better understood, and
the chosen laborers better cared for.

All hail to the good time at hand, which
is to usher in, through tribulation, purer,
brighter, happier conditions for the children
of men, — to be realized, in a measure, even
by some of those who now tread the earth.
But even with willingness of mind, it would,
with rare exceptions, require more than one
generation to overcome the power of inheritance and habit, so as to live fully up to the
higher law in all things. There must be
sincere conviction, and then long and patient
striving, ere the goal can be reached. It
can and will be attained, not by any startling
operation of divine power, though the development may be comparatively rapid, after

all these centuries of preparation. It must be by growth of the Christ principle in the human heart. The kingdom, God's kingdom, is coming through better men and better women; and these must be developed through better living, out of *truer, holier birthrights* than fall to the lot of most of earth's children now.

Would that these words could reach the minds and hearts of all who remain stagnant in their old inherited conditions, too content with their spiritual riches to seek the wealth now offering to humanity through channels opened under the influences, though not all under the much-abused name, of modern Spiritualism! Let them not be too sure of their position, or shut their eyes to their lack of spiritual gifts—and to the many manifest proofs that they have hardly yet begun to receive the knowledge of God given to the world eighteen centuries ago! Again the voice of the Spirit cries out, "Woe unto you rich!" Woe unto you churches, that have builded costly monuments of faith and zeal, but for heavenly manna have gathered too much the lifeless chaff of creeds and dogmas, the empty husks of formal observance, with which to feed the

hungry souls crying to you for bread!
Regenerating humanity will not much longer
be held in bondage. Look to your treasures, and see that they bear the stamp of
God's own imprint, lest ye perish through
very poverty of spirit; while every human
home must become a house of prayer, and
every fireside an altar to the living God.

ARTICLE V.

Spiritualism a Searching Power.

No escape from Judgment.— Spiritual perception not of the Intellect.— Guidance of the spirit possible for all.— It gives reality to spirit.— The Marriage Relation.— Joining of hands.— To spiritualize the natural, the need and work of the hour.

THE foregoing article offers a brief exposition of the work, progress, and outlook of Modern Spiritualism. Its necessary limits exclude much having important bearing upon the meaning and value of the new conditions.

Spiritualism, as there claimed, by its direct testimonies, throws light upon the path in which men have been groping,— makes clearer to their vision the impediments to their progress,— shows anew the truth and the life by which they can be brought to better development, and, in general, calls them to come up higher. It brings a power that tries all conditions. The companionships of earth-life try our hearts and minds, affecting their action in daily experience; the influence of those about us, unseen by the natural eye, is trying our lives yet more, and in ways little realized, until some action declares our states. From their searching scrutiny there can be no concealment, and from the judgment of our inner selves, no escape; while good angels would lead all men to be, in humbleness of spirit, children of God, whose love, whose wisdom, whose power, seem now ready to pour upon those who will receive, as never before vouchsafed. Through recognition of the spirit agency, both mind and heart are the more readily quickened. With deep desire and earnest prayer in heart and mind, the doors of the spirit may be opened, so that none but heavenly visitors can enter.

The subtle forces engaged in the manifestation of spiritual or supernatural phenomena, whether of high or low degree, have conditions peculiarly their own, and are subject to laws not fully understood as yet, but which are, nevertheless, as fixed as the laws regulating natural phenomena. In one regard, however, there is a law common to the investigation of both natural and spiritual phenomena. It is true of science on the spiritual as on the natural plane, that no man can make *original* investigation unless his heart be filled with sincere love. Pure intellect can often follow up and seem to occupy the tracks of other minds which have preceded under the illumination of love ; but it cannot make sound, successful, original research under its own cold light alone. He who would find out God in things of the spirit must have the love of God in his heart. Doubtless, increasing knowledge of God in the mind quickens the heart's love and gives it direction, while it enlarges the sphere of its manifestation; but the love must be there to be quickened. The difference is wide between the inquiry of the mind alone into the facts and philosophy of spiritual or supernatural phenomena, and the seeking of the heart after pure spirituality in things of the spirit. The two need to be combined for attainment of the broad science of Modern Spiritualism.

Humble-mindedness is always an indispensable condition in this, as in every other inquiry into truth. The valley of humility lies ever before the mount of vision. The failure of many (so called) scientific investigations into the ordinary, external phenomena of Spiritualism has been instructive on this point. Coming to the examination with little love in their hearts, and to their lack of love adding pride of intellect, such inquirers have been baffled, and refused admission at the very outer gates of that portal which may open, according to the real desire of the seeker, up through the blessed angels to the very presence of God.

The claim of Spiritualism, that a new dispensation is opening to earth-life through its manifold agencies, has awakened a desire in the minds of many, by whom the phenomena cannot yet be accepted as veritable, to know the supposed relation of the new conditions, if true, to their old faith. Allusion has been made heretofore to what seemed to be the general relation of Spiritualism to Christianity. A closer relation will be found in the development and operation of the *spiritual perceptions* under these modern influences, which we would endeavor briefly to set forth.

Realization of spirit presence through physical manifestation — whether of the startling

character of recent "materializations," or of
the simpler kind — is not sufficient of itself to meet the craving of the soul to reach
up through the avenues of sense and liftings
of the spirit till it can find the Father; but
it is an important remove from the ordinary
material plane of life. The fact of being
face to face with a spirit on the other side of
the veil of time, once realized through personal experience, breaks utterly and forever
the spell of materiality, which has overgrown
the spiritual perceptions of humanity, and
made the average conception of spiritual
things so vague and unsatisfactory. That
spell once broken, the way is opened to
earnest seekers for recognition of mental and
spiritual impressions from invisible sources,
leading to a development of the spiritual perceptions which will come gradually, and, with
steadfast desire in the mind for the highest
and best, will prove to be reliable and good.

To have the spiritual perceptions thus
developed is to realize far more than the possibility and fact of spirit communing and intercourse. It is to have mind and heart opened
to a recognition of spiritual elements and
conditions, in a manner and to a degree that
can hardly be understood, and certainly not

enjoyed by those living wholly on the natural
plane, however pure their lives, or even spiritual their desires. It is the opening of a
new sense, but with wider range than any and
all the natural senses, and more exquisite in
its varied enjoyments, by as much as things
of the spirit are above things of the natural
world. Spiritualizing the natural senses, each
in their special direction, to perception of
spiritual sights and sounds, to recognition of
finer magnetisms in the touch of angel
hands, to unwonted satisfaction and enjoyment in the elements of simple food, to the
scent of richest fragrance from flowers of
heaven, brought by loving friends, perhaps
not visibly, — for such spiritual openings are
not, as yet, always active together, — the development of spiritual perceptions leads to
intelligent acquirement and realization of the
various *gifts of the spirit*, of which the Christian world has read so often and understands
so little. In addition to these comes now
the possibility of unfoldment and insight
into all the spiritual elements underlying the
whole natural world.

Such experience leads yet further to a
guidance within the spirit, which may thus,
by a process of growth, learn to draw from

the very depths of God's love and wisdom,
through the manifold agencies of his appointment, both on the natural and spiritual planes.
Such guidance is not an after-recognition
following experience, but an influence more
or less present to the consciousness, and
quickly responsive to the seeking of the spirit
for right direction in every movement of
thought, prompting and leading in every act.
It calls for no mere passive state, inviting the
mental faculties to listless inactivity. On
the contrary, the more developed those faculties may be, the larger is the range of action
for the guidance; only they must be held in
ever humble willingness to be led by the
divine hand, while eager to do all their part
in carrying out the promptings. The reason
will not fail to throw its light upon any and
every work to which man is called, and check
the folly of blind impulse, while it waits
upon the spiritual man to find what the work
to do is. The more developed and active
the reasoning powers, the more ready is the
divine hand to help, when sought after in
true humbleness. Said the voice in the old
fable, " Put thy shoulder to the wheel; then
call on Jupiter, and he will help thee." But,
while not requiring a mere passive state, the

spirit must be calm within, or it cannot perceive the promptings aright, nor hear the
still, small voice correctly. The waters must
be unruffled, if they would receive and reflect
the heavenly images without distorted lines.
Impatient zeal may be as great a hindrance
as over-confidence in the intellectual faculties.

Recognizing and grateful for the part which
spirit agency takes in such direction, the
earnest seeker will find the possibility and
actual fulfilment of those words of the
Psalmist, " He shall give his angels charge
over thee, lest thou dash thy foot against a
stone." He must not be discouraged if the
impressions of such guidance come faintly at
first. Most things which grow well grow
slowly, and from small beginnings. Neither
should he falter when the promptings lead to
painful experience, except to question the
sincerity of his purpose and the reasonable-
ness of his conduct. If the asking has been
true, the result will show that the guidance
has been good in the lessons of life which
were needed, and could come only through
such teaching. Thus Spiritualism, by awakening and educating the spiritual perceptions,
makes clearer and broader to this age of development the way by which, with earnest

striving and patient waiting, humanity may rise higher and higher in spiritual attainment, co-working with God and the angels, until at last all its actions shall be outworkings of the Divine Spirit, and the promises of old be fulfilled.in the life of every child of earth.

If the spiritual state thus to be attained appear the same as that considered in Christian churches as the legitimate result of true Christian development, it follows that Spiritualism is not antagonistic to Christianity. It is, indeed, its latter-day coadjutor; and, while bringing the two-edged sword of truth, like Christianity, it comes to fulfil, not to destroy. To the minds of hasty observers, the work of Spiritualism has been a puzzle, if not an offence, in the varied character of its communications and teachings, as a whole, compared with the single purpose of spiritual unfoldment manifested in the Christian dispensation. But the way opened to one must need be opened to all the spirit-spheres, which thus bring the operative power of judgment to every condition of earth-life, and in a measure come to judgment themselves. Through all the various teachings and communication of things spiritual, however, the higher angels have been and are

instilling and directly communicating lessons
of wisdom and elements of divine love from
the Christ-sphere, supported by such assur-
ances as conditions have permitted, even to
the surpassing sense of peace believed to be
of the very Christ. Thus the promises of
old are being fulfilled, though not in ways
expected ; and, though men have hardly yet
begun to live up to the truth that was and is
in Christ Jesus, the angel-bands are bringing
to earth-life new elements and ushering in a
new era, which, in its outworkings, shall fulfil a new and yet larger Messianic hope, to
meet the spiritual needs of advancing humanity.

Admitting gratefully the advantage of
their starting-point, by birth and education
in a Christian community, many Spiritualists
have found it due to the truth to declare
that they are directly indebted to Spiritualism — beginning with the alphabet of
physical manifestations, the rappings and
table-tippings — for a new life, which is to
their old life as light to darkness. The actuality of their own spirit — of spirit life as
distinct from the natural life, and of spirit
existence in the life to come, was so vague
to their comprehension, before the light of

Modern Spiritualism dawned upon their minds, that they could get no real hold of any things of the spirit. "Our Father" was comparatively an "unknown God," whom they "worshipped ignorantly;" and Jesus, a distant friend, whose life they could admire, but whose great love they could neither fully receive nor reciprocate. The truths of pure, unsectarian, gospel Christianity are, indeed, the foundation of all true life, by showing the Father and spiritualizing the moral law in those commands, "Thou shalt love the Lord with all thy heart, and thy neighbor as thyself," on which "hang all the Law and the Prophets." Spiritualism, in its appointed time, comes to give a reality to spirit, which could hardly be known before, and helps the mind to a better understanding and the heart to a more living sense of God as spirit, who is to be "worshipped in spirit and in truth." Knowing that Spiritualism has come a helper to many, substantially in the manner described, we cannot but add our conviction that an honest admission would show to very many more a similar need, calling for similar help, in these days when materialism has so overshadowed and imperceptibly grown

into the lives of all. It was hardly to be
expected, indeed, that man could take such
leaps in material development and make no
discoveries on the spiritual side of his life.
Such a one-sided strain could not long be
borne ; the equilibrium of his being would
be destroyed. Closing in the spiritual perceptions and stunting spiritual growth, the
whirl of excitement on the material plane in
modern times would have driven mankind
mad, if some such additional help had not
broken in from the skies to save them.

With the spiritual perceptions opened, the
most practical life becomes spiritualized, as
every life should be. Spirit mediumship, as
we have before intimated, according to its
character and degree of sensitiveness, requires
more or less relief from the ordinary pressure of practical duties, a certain setting
apart for the special service ; but Spiritualism, in its simple opening of the spiritual
perceptions, which is its normal work with all
true seekers, will lead no man or woman
away from the duties which practical life
demands at their hands. Material interests
have their divinely appointed laws, which
must be obeyed, and which, under true guidance of the spirit, will not be ignored.

Spiritual development cannot contravene these laws, but only operate to give them their most beneficent expression. To the humblest laborers the divine guidance can come to lead and cheer them on, so that, in the most commonplace details, they may feel themselves to be co-workers with God. But, until the whole of humanity is opened to the new life, there must be struggle, and perhaps suffering, for those whose light shines upon darkness that " comprehendeth it not." Through all the weary centuries has this guidance been seeking to lead and help man in his struggles for development; but it has failed of due recognition and accomplishment, because the diviner elements of his being have been so covered over with the scales of ignorance on the one hand, or of intellectual conceit on the other, as to allow only a partial approach of the manifold agencies of the ever-waiting spirit of God.

Laboring to raise mankind out of the sloughs into which they have fallen through ignorance and indifference, the higher agencies of Spiritualism are not deterred from their work by false delicacy or artificial considerations. Viewing man in his twofold aspect, — the spiritual and the natural,— they seek to make known what are the elements which have their life wholly on the natural plane of his being, and what on the spiritual, placing the spiritual always in the supremacy. Looking thus at the marriage relation, alluded to in our previous article, right understanding of which lies at the very foundation of social science, though to some minds it is almost a forbidden subject, it appears that on the natural plane marriage springs from the attraction of magnetisms; and that far too often these are the controlling, if not the only, forces actuating human mating. These do give rise to emotions of love; but such emotions, being from their origin wholly on the natural plane, are selfish, and, like all other selfish promptings, seek selfish gratification, leading to fruits of selfishness. In every true marriage there is spiritual love also, which may be known by its seeking the good of another rather than its own gratification, and by not being exhausted, but rather growing, through expression. Human mating being comparatively free from natural limitations, the selfish promptings, which are equally strong in the natural man as in all other forms of life below him, must be held in restraint by the spiritual man.

Out of his freedom comes man's special responsibility, in this relation as in all others, of enlightened self-control, which must look to *divine purpose* for its direction and strength. Constrained by the higher love, the marriage relation is lifted to its proper plane; and obedience to divine law, as shown in purpose, becomes both possible and easy.

Such constraint is no mere asceticism. Sincere inquiry will make plain what the purpose and law are, and what are the obstacles to obedience, as well as the occasion for promulgation of these views in the present average state of the marriage relation : obedience in this regard being an indispensable step in the progress of humanity toward establishing spiritual supremacy in all the relations of life, — that essential basis of God's " kingdom on earth," for which the centuries have been praying that it come "as in heaven." It is due to Spiritualism that this call for higher life should be accredited to its influence and suggestion, in happy contrast with ideas which, at the opening of its work, have obtained a limited hold upon some of its more forth-putting believers, and left a temporary stain upon its fair name, that would not have been possible but for

the weakness of old conditions thus brought
to judgment.

Marriage has been defined to be the effort
of spirit to ultimate itself in form.   It is
plain that the quality of the ultimation must
depend upon the character of the spirit involved, whether that be on the plane of
pure, unselfish love, or on the lower plane
of selfish gratification.   Let true spiritual
marriage underlie the natural mating, with
the life on the natural plane directed by a
holy desire to build up and sustain the body
as a temple for the indwelling of a pure
spirit, and the true intent of the marriage
relation in earth-life will be wrought out in
such lives, such homes, and such beautiful
offspring as humanity are not often blessed
with now.   The subject is momentous, and
demands the fullest consideration.   Spiritualism proclaims in general that better social
conditions are at hand, waiting only for man's
willingness to welcome them.   This cannot
be until these grave matters are taken into
the thoughts, and worked out in the lives
of women and men.   In the name of God,
pure Spiritualism demands that the divine
purpose in all the relations of life be sought
and followed out.   Co-working with God

and his agencies, it rests with man to help on the coming of his kingdom.

In this connection we would allude briefly to the joining of hands at their gatherings, to which the attention of Spiritualists, as well as of outside observers, has been seriously called. The joining of hands on such occasions has sometimes proved to be more than the old conditions could bear, and selfishness has crept in to mar and prevent the otherwise harmonizing interchange of magnetic influence. Like the love-feasts of the early Christians, those meetings have tried the old conditions in the balance of spiritual intent, and too often found them wanting. The results are ground for argument against entering into such relations unguardedly, and do show the error of joining in promiscuous gatherings, where the motives of all present may not be equally sincere and unselfish; but they furnish no reason for refusing to join in the seeking, where a sincere purpose is known to control. There ought to be no safer or better place for this joining of hands in spiritual seeking than in the home circle. Try the spirits honestly, devoutly, reverently toward God, and there need be no fear of evil consequences, while the way may thus

be opened to the highest spiritual unfoldment.

The disposition of seekers in Modern
Spiritualism to be contented with witnessing
supernatural phenomena, without following
up to the higher things of the spirit, was to
be expected at first. By degrees, a larger
and deeper interest has been and will doubtless be yet more awakened; while experience
is showing that those words of the Apostle,
"Though I have the gift of prophecy, and
understand all mysteries and all knowledge,
. . . and have not charity [love], I am
nothing," are as true now as when they
were spoken. To *spiritualize* the *natural*,
as Jesus labored to spiritualize the moral,
so that the divine spirit and uses which underlie all things in the natural shall have due
recognition and full expression, is the work
of Modern Spiritualism, — not to astonish
by external wonders, or merely gratify curiosity about the conditions of life in other
spheres of existence. Heretofore, when spirit
forces have drawn near to earth-life, the
manifestations of their presence and power
have seemed marvellous. As the work of
development goes on, and harmonious relations are established, with open communion

and communication between the natural and the spiritual worlds, these manifestations will no longer be exceptional or in any sense strange. The call for signs and wonders will cease ; and humanity, drawing nearer to God, will move on, happy in fulfilling its varied part in the ever-repeating miracle of daily life. Such are the promises of the New Dispensation.

ARTICLE VI.

Unfoldment of the New Era.

Method of procedure.—The new era one of spiritual opening.—Its quickening causes the turmoil of the times. — Inspiration better understood. — Causes retarding progress.—Foremost, ignorance and disobedience of Law in the marriage relation. —Too much selfishness, too little Love.—False shame. — Errors in food. — Real needs of the physical.—Spiritualism a source of consolation to the afflicted.—Individuality its first requirement.

A New Dispensation! These momentous words have been written under full conviction — based upon facts of external observation and inner experience — that this world of ours, after its long and weary centuries of preparation, is entering, has indeed entered, upon a new era of development; something more than the growth which is always going on,— differing from what has gone before by discrete degree, though resting upon antecedent epochs as its necessary foundation.

With all the recent rapid development on the material plane of earth-life, the new era is pre-eminently one of spiritual unfoldment. Modern Spiritualism cannot be said to constitute, or to embrace, the fulness of this dispensation; it is rather the broad way through which the wonders and the glories of the new life are opening upon earth. How far the facts and experience on which this conviction rests can be shared by all, depends largely upon the receptiveness of each. As of old, men having eyes may not see, and ears may not hear, the signs of the times; or hearing and seeing, they may not comprehend their import, though unable to find other satisfactory interpretation.

The method of procedure has been in establishing the basis on which the higher manifestations could rest, through the evidence given on the natural plane, of the actuality and nearness of spirit identities existing and at work on the other side of the veil, — which veil is every day becoming less and less obstructive to communication between the natural and the spirit spheres: and by the inspiration and very apparent quickening work of these spirit forces, which, whether recognized or not, are moving the world of humanity so potently now to new thought and action. History tells of other similar operations of the spirit-spheres upon earth-life; but these have been less potent and extensive than now, when the preparations are more complete, the conditions more ready to receive the great impulse, more ripe for development. No other view of our times furnishes rational explanation of the turmoil which, for many years, has prevailed over the face of our globe, through individual, social, and national experience, showing such universal quickening. Modern Spiritualism furnishes a key to the mysteries of modern life, on whatever side they may be examined, — the very forces of nature feeling the impulse, and startling humanity into inquiry of the whence and the whither, as never before. To some minds, alarmed by the apparent quickening of evil, the moral world seems to be hopelessly rushing to destruction in deeds of wickedness; while others rejoice in the more than equal outgrowth of the better elements combining so manifestly to meet and overcome the rising evil. Such spiritual conflict found vent in our own Civil War, with its manifold experiences, including the horrors of Andersonville prisons and the mercies of sanitary commissions, — each and all working out and illustrating the purification through which men and nations have to pass before rising to the baptism of the new birth into a new and more blessed epoch.

That such an event as the opening of a new era should come in the secret manner which has thus far characterized this spiritual epoch, is in accord with the law of all development, which is from within outward. In the secret chambers of earth, hidden from the light of the sun and the eye of man, the seeds of all growing things have ever been laid to germinate. Only in the higher councils could the processes and times of the new unfoldment be known or anticipated.

We have said that the new era is one preeminently of the spirit. External motives, having regard wholly to material ends, will give way to the higher motives of inner purpose and use. This idea has been proclaimed by inspired teachers, and accepted by well-ordered minds, as the true rule of man's life, through all the centuries of his slow development. The time has come when it must hold full sway, and mankind cease to be ruled by the things they now think to possess. Material development has been a necessary antecedent. The spiritual elements could find small opportunity for growth until the creature necessities of food, raiment, and dwelling place were provided. Man's first efforts have been to procure these; and easily has he become so absorbed in their acquirement as to measure the success of his life by the amount and character of such possessions. Development of power over material elements has been and is the aim of our education. With the child's mind so directed, the man could hardly fail to be absorbed in the pursuit, which is well as a means but not as an end. The new era is to be characterized by material development for its uses only. The larger the use, the higher the value of the possession. Radical inquiry into all the uses of life already marks the times, under the great quickening through spirit influence. Not that the spirit-spheres do all the labor, making the individual life of earth only machine-work under their hands. Individuality is rather to grow more developed and pronounced, each human being feeling more

and more the responsibility of filling his
part in the economy of God's kingdom.
Inspired by new thought and power from
above, humanity will move on under the
quickening impulse and the promptings of a
great purpose, until raised to its proper plane
of spiritual unfoldment.

The testimony of Spiritualism upon the
subject of Inspiration has been interesting
and valuable, leading to more intelligent understanding and a more rational philosophy
of its operation than was possible to this
materialistic age, or perhaps to any age, before the advent of the full modern spiritual
phenomena. We say testimony, for it is
not inference or argument. The evidence
offered, and the uniform declaration from
the spirit-spheres, unite to establish the fact
that God works through individualized agencies in the mysteries of inspiration, as in all
the other works and ways wherein man finds
manifestation of His presence and power.
The difference between the inspiration from
the spirit-spheres, and that which proceeds
from the more apparent influences of earth-
life, is one of degree rather than of method.
The various forms of the latter are so familiar that they do not attract attention unless

manifested in very striking ways or on great
occasions, though wonderful in their simplest
form. The power of one mind over many,
through word, look, or act, the charm of
oratory, the quickening flash of the eye, the
high purpose of noble deeds, the mere presence of a great man,— these all operate with
inspiring influence. Well-spoken words are
taken up and passed from mouth to mouth,
carrying a power with every repetition, till
the world rings with their inspiring sound.
There is inspiration even from inanimate
things, quickening every receptive life and
prompting often to new thought and action.
By a similar, but more direct and complete
process, intelligences from the spirit-spheres
inspire receptive minds with thoughts already
fashioned, — sometimes putting the very
words into the mouths of the mediums held
in more or less unconscious trance ; or they
quicken the receptive brain to its own fash-
ioning of thought. Thus what has been
accepted among men as divine inspiration,
is shown and declared to have been given
through individualized beings, angels of light
and love, bringing heavenly truths from
their heavenly homes to help and bless our
mundane sphere. The familiar forms of

spirit-control for purposes of communication, together with the manifestation of high inspirational powers in various forms of mediumship, have educated Spiritualists to accept this as the method of inspiration which, upon reflection, will be found to commend itself to the understanding, and to lead to a comprehensive philosophy of the whole subject; though it does militate, at first painfully, against the preconceived ideas which have been handed down from generation to generation of earth's children; children still, they are, in the hands of the All-Father, however enabled, through development, to comprehend more and more of his wondrous works and ways.

In olden time, " Thus saith the Lord " were the familiar words used by persons touched by the fire from above. In later days, down to our own time, that which has seemed to be the " voice of God " has been heard within the inner consciousness of quickened minds. Such inspiration, whether of the past or the present, is one and the same in method. Angel-voices have spoken, and spirit-powers, high and low, have inspired, since man's life on earth began. We know not, perhaps we can never know, just

where the inspiration begins; or draw the
line between the thought generated by the
action of our own minds, and thoughts instilled directly or indirectly from other
spheres. We do know however that, of
old and now, the character of the inspiration turns largely upon the development
and motive of the person seeking and receiving it. The voice of God, through his
manifold agencies in the spirit-spheres, comes
to man as inspiration; and, through all these
agencies, the selfish elements of the natural
plane — which may still hang about the
spirits who have gone out from visible earth-
life steeped in those elements — are ever
contending with the higher and more spiritual for supremacy, — ever ready to offer
their enticing promises of advantage and
pleasure, even to the eating of the forbidden
fruit of the " tree of knowledge of good and
evil."

These voices, this inspiration of the spirit,
now as of old, must be brought to the bar
of individual judgment for determination of
their right or wrong, their wisdom or their
folly. This may be done by direct consideration of the promptings or teachings; or,
as has been largely necessary in the course of

human development up to this period, by
measuring the doctrine through the otherwise
recognized merit of the medium or teacher,
whose example and acknowledged development have given authority to his words.
There is no escape from this responsibility
of direct or indirect individual adjudication.
Spiritualists know, and have shown by the
outworking of their experience in this regard, — to their own misery often, as well as
to the present disparagement of their cause,
— how surely every spirit that comes to them,
whether through their own consciousness, or
voiced by others, must be " tried ; " how inspiration in every form must be weighed in
the balance of such truth as lies in each one
of us. The closest self-questioning and
weeding out of low motive have proved the
first, if not the only safeguard against grave
errors, which have been possible through
willingness to close the mind to the warnings
of the monitor within, sometimes against the
plainest dictates of common-sense, when
seemingly authoritative suggestions have come
to encourage the doing of what would be
pleasant, or in accord with our own thinking,
rather than what would be independently right
and wise. The unhappy Pocassett child-

slayer heard what seemed to him the voice
of God, as did the assassin, Guiteau. Very
possibly there were voices, promptings of the
spirit, mingled with their own unbalanced
thinkings. It is all one and the same method of inspiration ; its source and special
direction turning, in their cases, as in others
of like character, upon their own mental and
moral weakness and folly, — making them,
personally, fit subjects for commiseration and
restraint, while their deeds call for utter condemnation. Such appears to have been,
from the first, the method of divine working
in this regard, leading by devious ways to
the grand result of human development
through experience. Acknowledged leaders,
seers of their day, have in the past been lifted
to the heights supreme, from which they
could see and report the truths unfolded to
their lofty aspirations. Modern Spiritualism
would have all its children attain these heights,
and live rejoicing on the plane of spiritual
unfoldment which has been thus proclaimed,
from the mountain-tops of human vision, to
be the ultimate destiny of the race.

The development which receives the
highest inspiration is not necessarily based
upon what has been heretofore considered

the highest culture; though culture, if true, is no bar, but rather an aid, to inspiration. "The pure in heart shall see God;" and this may or may not come of culture. Culture has in the past tended to ruts and limits. Developing the mind in some directions, it has closed it in others, so that new light could hardly find entrance. The uneducated fishermen were called first; and then the learned Paul was broken into the service. Again and again have things of the spirit been " hid from the wise and the prudent." With progressing development these conditions must change. The culture now opening to earth-life, largely through the inspiration and quickening from the spirit-spheres, is to be wider and truer than that of the past. The false, because wholly external motive of life, will give way to a spiritual unfoldment and supremacy; so that the more the culture, the better and more enlarged the channels of communication, the better and higher the inspiration from the influences, God's messengers, ever waiting to draw near to the children of earth, as the way opens for them and conditions attract them.

It will be seen that this broad philosophy

of inspiration includes within its scope all
forms of divination from the earliest ages,
many of which have been such stumbling-
blocks to what has been claimed as the common-sense of the materialistic age now
drawing to its close. It reconciles the difficulties which have so often perplexed the
studies of the scholar and theologian in this
regard ; and — though it may not lead them
to send embassies in hope of finding and re-
viving the oracles of old, or to give too
willing credence to the stories of divine response through angel, ghost, or sprite, so
abundant in the past — it will surely help
them to more correct estimate of what has
so often been set down as ignorant credulity,
and to find it no longer necessary to stultify
the wise and good of past generations, in
order to give any place to the statements of
spiritual intervention in the affairs of men,
handed down through history and myth.

But with all the development of modern
civilization, there is much wanting before
man can receive the teachings of the inspiration now waiting to lead him up to the
height of his great calling. Foremost among
the causes which retard his progress and
higher attainment is declared to be igno-

rance and disobedience of divine law in the marriage relation, to the true culture of which we would again allude as lying at the foundation of social science.

More and more the beautiful outworking or the terrible power of heredity are recognized among the most potent causes of man's weal or woe. There is a call yet more to recognize the power for good or evil in the birthright of every human being, which comes not of ancestral origin only, but is the direct result of true or false conditions in each particular parentage. Out of the heart are the issues of life; and most assuredly out of the marriage relation, before aught else, spring the tendencies which determine the starting-point of every new-born life. This familiar thought demands such consideration now as it has never yet received, for the establishment of a basis in the coming development. There must be cultivated first a truer and more general desire for knowledge in this momentous regard. By degrees the wrongs may become more apparent of themselves, and be slowly eradicated through independent action of each sincere mind and willing heart. But conditions so established through ignorance

and the predominance of selfish life on the
natural plane, so long rooted in the broad
field of humanity, must need be, in a measure, forcibly ejected, before they can be
planted out by the better life, under the
knowledge brought through suffering; and
the sooner the work of removal is begun,
the speedier will be the coming of the long-
desired kingdom.   Man's freedom to break
the divine law indicated in purpose has given
him opportunity to know, through experience, the bitter fruits of disobedience.   Let
him cease now to make that freedom his
poor excuse, and turn it rather into noble
opportunity for willing obedience, by which
alone he can become master of his lower
nature, and in the highest sense a law unto
himself, through perfect accord with the
Good Father's will and purpose.   As never
before, angel messengers are pressing this
momentous subject upon the minds of the
men and women of to-day.   Like the voice
of God again sounding through the Garden,
is the call summoning man to answer if he
has been true in this most sacred relation.
Shall shame, through past disobedience, still
force him to hide from the Great Presence?
Let him, rather, penitently study the broken

injunction, and, with the wisdom gathered
out of suffering, humbly re-enter at the once
flaming gates,— through his obedience no
longer a barrier,— and seek to attain that
felicity, handed down among all peoples and
from all time since he became a sojourner
upon earth, as his true birthright. Paradise
gained or regained, it matters not, if only its
blessed possibility be reached!

It is interesting to observe how, through
predominance of the natural or selfish love,
comes the sense of possession, which actuates
all mating among the lower animals, and
shows itself in man through the passion
of jealousy. This is plainly for the protection and welfare of animal life on the natural
plane; but for man is needed only so long
as his life is ordered on that plane. When
human life is raised to its spiritual standard,
so that men and women, through subjection
of the natural to the spiritual love, can rule
themselves, the need of this selfish element,
this sense of possession in love, disappears.
The marriage relation, entered into with
consentient attraction and impulse on both
the natural and spiritual planes,— which increase in power with true use and wise experience,— becomes a durable bond that

needs no such jealous protection. The
selfish sense of possession gives place to a
proper sense of belonging that leaves no
opportunity for doubt, and would afford no
encouragement to selfish approaches from
without. Love between men and women,
thus held in the service of God, is free for
other and wide expression, not limited to
the mated relation, which will help to keep
that relation fresh and strong in its own
proper bounds, instead of being dragged out
in selfish confinement — leading to indifference, if not repulsion, as it too often now is.
The sacred injunction, *Love one another*, no
longer restrained by fear of selfish misrule,
would be followed in all the social relations
with such beautiful adaptations and healthful
results, on both the natural and spiritual
planes, as has been possible only in exceptional instances during these eighteen hundred years of slow development of the
Christ ideal. In such way has the true
gospel of Modern Spiritualism come to fulfil, not to destroy. That this individual
ruling of the life, through supremacy of the
spiritual love, has no conflict with human
law is readily seen. When the marriage relation is thus conducted the statutes regu-

lating it will be no impediment, and the laws
of divorce will happily become dead-letter
laws ; as those against theft and murder are
dead letters to all whose lives are up to the
Christian standard of love to God and man.

The evil to be overcome, being deep-
seated, demands radical treatment. The
work of prevention must begin with the
young. Children must be educated to accept natural things naturally, and ever with
the pure spirit to which all things are pure.
The ideas of false shame, now so generally
inculcated, must give place to a desire for
holiness before God and man. Let them be
taught to look upon clothes no longer as the
covering of nakedness and shame, but rather
as climatic necessities, and protection from
injury and unwholesome approaches,—while
still calling for proper interest in appearance,
to make that pleasant as may be to others.
Indifference to the decencies of life is not
involved in such idea of dress. Taught
that the body is but the clothing of the
spirit, let children learn to cherish it with religious desire for its best development and
the highest and best use of its powers ; and
in turn to care for the clothing of the body,
with the desire foremost to accommodate it

to its chief uses. Before God, and in the eye of the pure spirit, there is no such condition as nakedness, in the low sense suggested in false shame, resulting from false education and false living.

By the removal of false shame through right education, so that all natural relations shall be looked upon with the purity of mind that knows not shame, and with the subjection of the natural to the spiritual love through proper culture of both, most momentous ends will be accomplished. Evils which are now the despair of the wisest philanthropy will find their only effective prevention, and coming generations will everywhere rise up to call their parents blessed.

Among the obstacles to attaining the new life, spirit messengers allude often to errors in food. This leads to the general subject of appetite. Given to the animal kingdom for the purpose of keeping up the life of the body, and continuing the races to their appointed uses and ends, the appetites of the flesh have ascended to man, through his relation to that kingdom, and in the state to which they had been developed prior to his life upon earth. In these appetites, as in

other respects, the comparative anatomy of
body and spirit, through the animal races,
leads up to man. Among the brute animals,
to whom is given no power from generation
to generation of improving their natural
states, — though all the while they have been
elaborating the elements of earth through
their several organisms, each after their kind,
— the appetites are restrained by fixed conditions. But for man, called to a higher
destiny, these natural restraints are removed,
his range for possible indulgence of appetite
being almost without limit. Uniting in his
organism, physically and spiritually, all the
elements of earth-life, man, the microcosm,
is gifted with power, and therewith called to
subdue these elements, and in his turn to
raise them in their various forms to their
highest development. As he finds himself
opposed by the forces of nature in subduing
the surface of the earth, whence has come,
through difficulty and struggle, much of his
present external progress, so in his corresponding labor to subdue, develop, and elevate the creature elements, — handed up to
him through the whole animal kingdom, to
be perfected in his body and spirit, — he
must meet and overcome difficulty and op-

position before he can attain "the prize of
his high calling." Thus in man's own being
at last, would seem to be centred the "conflict of the ages," begun in the war of elements, when form first sprang out of chaos,
and to be ended only when his destiny is
fulfilled. Having divine uses, the appetites
of the flesh — in their natural condition, and
legitimate development through the animal
kingdom — are good, though selfish. In
man they are good, and in their action
crowned with a proper joy, so long as they
are held by the divine principle within him
to true uses and ends. But when perverted
from their true uses and allowed unrestrained
indulgence, — made possible through the
free agency, without which he would not be
in the image of God, — these appetites fall
into states of hell, and carry with them the
victims of their power.

Much, then, must depend upon the right
selection of food, as well as upon its temperate use. That the human race will in the
coming time find all its food in the grains,
fruits, and herbs, is not questioned. Many
facts of to-day point to this end. It is true
that the fibrin of animal flesh is found
chemically to be the gluten of the grains ;

but the gluten is raised one step in the progress of being by passing into the animal life, and so attains a quickening, heating, febrile power in flesh meat, which tends to over-stimulate and corrupt man's true health, however much habit and his present average development seem to demand, and perhaps for a time longer really do need it. Again, argument has been drawn in favor of animal food from the constitution of man's body, and especially from his teeth. It is claimed that his canine teeth indicate capacity for, and so need of, animal food; but here, again, *ultimate purpose*, on which rests the law of the new life, is shown in the canine being more than matched by the other teeth and the whole *set together upon an even line*, requiring a *harmonious* use for them all. Can this use be fulfilled by eating meat? The grains and the fruits, in their natural states as prepared by man, call into exercise all the teeth, including the canine, but they do not tend to encourage and keep in its natural qualities the canine element, as the feeding on flesh meat, the natural canine food, must. Taken as it is, the canine race can hardly live without its natural food, as indicated by its teeth ; but the canine element, as it exists

in man, can be sufficiently fed without flesh
meat. It is in man — as including all creature elements below him — that the possibilities of the lion eating grass, and the wolf
lying down with the lamb, may be fulfilled ;
while the original creatures themselves must
disappear from the face of the earth, their
work accomplished. " Paradise Regained "
will be satisfied with that primitive provision,
whatever its source, " Behold, I have given
you every herb bearing seed which is upon
the face of all the earth, and every tree in
the which is the fruit of a tree yielding seed;
to you it shall be for meat; and to every
beast of the earth and to every fowl of the air
and to every thing that creepeth upon the
earth, wherein there is life, I have given every
green herb for meat." Already a suggestion
of the coming time in this regard may be
found in the difference of feeling with which
refining humanity can pluck an ear of corn
and thank God for it, while it would shrink
with abhorrence from plunging the knife
into the living creature, whose flesh it still
craves and for a while may yet require.

A more interesting topic perhaps to the
general reader, and one of importance to

[1] Genesis i. 29, 30.

those who have known nothing of Spiritualism other than little-credited reports of its
phenomena, is the source of consolation,
real and available to all, opened through its
simplest manifestations. The aspect of death
is so changed through their acceptance, so
robbed of its terror, made so beautiful in the
absolute assurance of the new birth, — not
into a Plutonic kingdom of night, nor into
a far-off region of light whence no message
of love can return, but into a nearer realm
of spirit-life, to which the avenues of approach and communication are no longer
closed. The consolations of religious trust
are much and many; but they cannot fill the
void in the aching heart as can one word —
nay, one tiny rap — that assures of the near
presence of the loved and seemingly lost.
Not that any form of spirit manifestation
can wholly fill up the void caused by death,
or fully replace the magnetisms of the bodily
presence, the living elements of physical life
which are removed when the spirit puts off its
earthly habiliment; but to the cry so often
going out, " Give me one word, one touch,
one look " from the dear departed child, parent, brother, friend, Spiritualism does offer a
consoling response such as can come in no

other way; and it is as legitimate to find this comfort from the sources now opened as it is to avail of any of the alleviations of human suffering which the development of knowledge has brought, or — with the good Father's blessing and help — will yet be discovered for the ills of earth, ere they are removed through the better conditions now at hand and promised.

In closing we would once more touch upon the subject of Individuality, that there may be no misapprehension of what has been written of the continued influence exercised over human lives by the spirit-spheres. Real as that influence is, yet there is no escape from the responsibility of every child of earth to see to it that his life is well ordered out of the purpose of his own will and thought. Led, as he may be unawares, to lines of conduct not of his original seeking, the responsibility is to hold his purpose of well-doing without swerving, and leave the shaping of his life in such measure to circumstances and the unseen influences, in connection with his own desire and purpose, as may be allotted to him.

> "There's a divinity that shapes our ends,
> Rough-hew them how we will,"

and these unseen influences have much to
do in the shaping; but never should man or
woman let the reins slip from their hands so
far as to lose the power of determining
between right and wrong, under the best
culture of conscience which they can attain,
and of restaining every prompting and
impulse that is not in accord with their
highest sense of right.   To be passive and
receptive to all that is good, but positive and
repellant to all that is wrong, is the plain
and safe rule of conduct.   Spiritualism shows
that the advantage of such self-direction and
control goes out and beyond to others, in
ways and to an extent little dreamed of
by those unacquainted with these modern
proofs of spirit presence.   Indeed, none of
us can know fully the power of our lives to
help the benighted on those other shores,—
who are waiting to be led out of blind conditions, consequent upon their own life-experiences,— by the influence of our conduct
and lives, which is ever operating in turn to
help or to hinder the " cloud of witnesses "
about us.   " Spirits in prison " there are on
that other side, waiting for the resurrection of
our spirits — yet in earth-life — from low desires and external seekings, which are holding

us and them in continuing bondage to things
of sense, when they and we should be free in
the service of the Good Father. The power
of example and influence is recognized in
earth-life, and is momentous for that alone;
but how much more momentous when this
wider area of possible influence is contem-
plated! Surely, if other motive were wanting, here is inducement enough to raise the
dying and the dead in spirit out of their low
conditions, their living sepulchres, to the new
life in the NEW ERA now opening.

THE PURITY AND DESTINY OF
MODERN SPIRITUALISM.

Third Series.

"Ist's Gottes Werk, so wird's bestehen —
Ist's Menchen Werk, wird's untergehen."

Is it God's Work, so shall it stand —
Is it Man's Work, it will go under.

Inscription on the statue of Martin Luther at Wittenberg.

THIRD SERIES.

1899.

PREFATORY NOTE.

To state the present aspect of Modern
Spiritualism, as seen by the writer; — to
show some of the inconsistencies of unbelief, remove some of its obstacles, and explain more fully the necessity of its phenomenal presentation, culminating in Materialization; — to state more forcibly the
power it has exercised and is still destined to
exert, through its various channels, upon
earth life in every grade, the recognition of
which seems so needful for reception of the
sympathy and aid it has to offer, as well as
to meet successfully the threatening approaches of its lower orders and elements; —
and last, but not least, to declare in a more
distinct and emphatic manner, the true relations between man and woman, which have

been shown to the writer as the very foundation of social science ; — the following three Articles have been added. They complete, in a measure, the scheme of treatment which seems to have been laid out from the first.

The writer is well aware that the claim of influence on the part of the spirit-spheres, herein made, can hardly be accepted at once, or without some inquiry into the phenomena in their very varied presentation. With the hope of arousing a new and enlightened interest in such inquiry, he has endeavored to present something of its many and varied aspects. How far short he has come of covering the whole ground, as it may be covered later by some more able hand, he is fully conscious.

ARTICLE VII.

Spiritualism a New Science.

Demonology, what is it? — Obstacles to inquiry and belief. — Inconsistencies of opponents. — Necessity of external phenomena. — Materialization described at length. — Exclusion of sunlight a necessity, — why. — Plainer manifestations to result from better conditions of inquiry. — Means to a greater end. — Mistaken opposition. — The First Spiritual Temple. — Continuing Inspiration from highest sources to be cultivated.

PERHAPS the word, " Demonology," for a caption would better suit the mental state of many readers of an article on Modern Spiritualism, and it might be a correct term, if the original signification of the word, " demon," were not so nearly obsolete; its current meaning being limited to bad or undeveloped spirits, instead of including the whole range of spirit beings, good, bad and indifferent. Webster's first definition of the word "demon," is : "A spirit or immaterial being holding a middle place between men and the celestial deities of the pagans." This was its original meaning. Such, doubtless, was the "*daimon*" of Socrates, as understood by his contemporaries. But the secondary and now popular meaning of demon has long been limited to " evil spirit." A pocket Worcester's dictionary gives for its only meaning, "an evil spirit, a devil; " and " Demonology " has in general been so appropriated by "the devil and his angels," that the very sound of the word has grown to be an offence to polite ears. By easy association these words have included, in the popular mind, all spirits who could control human beings, and demoniacal possession has been recognized as one of the factors in human conduct, when the equally possible influence or control of good spirits had, before the advent of Modern Spiritualism, come to be quite ignored. Among the obstacles to acceptance of the facts of Spiritualism, not the least has been this secondary meaning and use of the words "demon " and " demonology," by operating to discredit the claims of Spiritualists that good was to be found in the varied spiritual manifestations, and so leading to refusal of the whole phenomena. Indeed it would sometimes seem that if the early advocates of the new spiritual truths, in their endeavors to draw the attention of the religious world to the facts, had confined themselves to statements concerning the manifestations of the lower orders of spirits, they would have gathered more speedily a goodly company of inquirers, who would have been prompt to do God service by meeting and battling with the old enemy of man, and so might have unexpectedly found themselves encompassed about by angels of light, marshalled at the bidding of the Lord of Hosts to do his will in the work of uplifting humanity!

But these fifty or more years since the first announcement of the new conditions, through tiny raps in the little village of Hydesville, have shown such astounding growth and progress of the new philosophy, that its disciples have ceased, in great measure, the eager advocacy of its doctrines which was so natural at its advent; well assured from the progress attained, that a power higher and mightier than any ordinary human organization has been and is behind the movement, and will in good time bring it to fruition in the long promised kingdom of righteousness and peace. If the coming be " like a thief in the night," it may be welcomed yet the more as led on in mysterious ways by the Master hand, which so many now in the fold believe has been directing its approach from the beginning.

No one cause has tended more to impede a proper understanding and easy acceptance of Modern Spiritualism for the unbeliever, than the general desire for a spiritual presentation of the subject, when the age in which we live has made what may be called the natural presentation its only avenue of approach. This is no contradiction of ideas, though it may at first seem so in terms. By force of the material and intellectual development of the last few centuries, the human mind, before the advent of Spiritualism, had been reduced to a state of infancy as to the power of spiritual discernment, recognized as one of the gifts of the Spirit eighteen hundred and more years ago, so that it could only begin to be informed in that direction in a manner similar to that by which the human infant has to begin the awakening or acquirement of all its ideas, namely through the external senses. For most inquirers at the outset, any attempt at a spiritual presentation of Spiritualism has been practically useless, and must continue so, more or less, until a wider breach has been made in the walls of spiritual unbelief; and this breach is to be effected first and easiest through the avenue of the senses. Leaders in spiritual things of to-day offer no exception to this necessity, any more than they did eighteen or more centuries ago. Spirit life, like external or natural life, has its order of being and manifestation, its causes and effects, now beginning to be understood as a philosophy before little comprehended. Simple physical manifestations, with responsive intelligence, leading up gradually to the more recent full form materializations, have been the first method for all. From the necessity of the situation, then, any candid presentation of the subject in what may be called its natural, rather than its spiritual aspect is, at the outset of inquiry, entitled at least to patient consideration.

Another difficulty in the approach of Spiritualism, and not a slight one, has been the fact with which the inquirer is early confronted, that the " communion of saints," so long established as one of the tenets of the Christian church, *has its foundation* in *natural law ;* and that while taking its special direction from spiritual culture, it is possible only by virtue of the fundamental fact through which, in these latter days, the way has been opened to all denizens of the spirit-spheres ; showing, sometimes so sadly, that all who are ready to commune from the other side of the veil of time are not saints, any more than those on this side of the veil who have sought the communion.

Never has the power of education and habit in fixing mental action in grooves been more markedly illustrated than in the position of negation toward Spiritualism held by many who are nevertheless assured of and ready to avow their belief in the near presence and very possible influence of loved ones gone before. Welcoming the poetic strains that tell of such near presence, and reciting them often with spiritual fervor, their minds still shrink strangely from any possibility of the poetic fancies being changed into real presence manifest to the external senses, though plainly such external manifestation is the only avenue of near approach available, when the gift of discerning spirits is so utterly lost and well nigh ridiculed by the heads of the Christian church, though half believed in as something possible two thousand years ago. It is strange, indeed, that so many of the more educated classes should be unable to perceive that this closing of the spiritual vision precludes the possibility of the spirit communing they vaguely desire as something which they could accept; while they repel the manifestations upon the natural or sensual plane, on which alone they are now capable of recognizing the spirit presence.

Again the more cultured classes, as a whole, are open to the charge of utter inconsistency in their shrinking from what seems to them at first as desecration of their loved dead, in the apparent necessity of finding the avenues of communication open to them only through strangers and in strange places. The moment a suggestion is made that they need not go so far for the communing, if only they would open their own hearts and homes to the conditions necessary everywhere for development of spirit mediumship, they are quick to resent the proposal as almost an insult; thus directly repelling, with their utmost force of will, the very possibility of having communication opened anywhere but in places strange to them ! Possibly it has not

occurred to them that the spirit friends themselves, longing for direct interchange of love
and thought with dear ones left behind, sub-
mit to conditions not of their own choosing;
nay more, are often forced to avail of states
otherwise repulsive to them, in order to get
into any avenue of approach ; a pain and
struggle they might well be saved, if only
the home circle, within its consecrated cham-
ber, could be established under every roof.
They too would shrink from the strange con-
tacts, often unavoidable in the ordinary
seance rooms, as repugnant to their own refinement as to the most delicate sense of the
friends in the form. Happily there are
public mediums whose personal purity and
and conduct would of themselves be no impediment to the coming of any one from the
spirit-spheres, and the number of these
doubtless will increase ; but the mixed company of strangers must too often include
elements at least inharmonious with the
tender emotions which are called out upon
a loving message, or it may be upon the open
vision and substantial presence of a dear departed form. Many good people who still
deny the privilege of such communing in
any manner to themselves and their spirit

friends, and are often ready enough, had they the power, to prevent all others from the privilege, will be astonished at their error, as countless other tardy acceptors of the new truths have been, when their eyes are opened, and the new light has fairly dawned upon them.

But not without some effort, and it may be sacrifice, is the inquiry into these mysteries, as into any other truth to be instituted. The votaries of old science are not to be waited upon, as so many of them have been prone to think, by the powers directing the great movement from the spirit-spheres. They, too, must come upon their knees in the simplicity of a childlike, though never childish willingness to be taught whatever they may be found fit to receive, as the early votaries of Spiritualism have done ; and perhaps in time learn that what they have heretofore refused to accept, because seemingly contrary to established truth, is not in fact contrary to, but something beyond and in addition to their former knowledge. The laws of gravitation, for instance, are not changed or contravened in the new manifestations of external force ; but new powers are introduced not hitherto known or recognized as factors in the great problem of mundane development. There is a science of these new forces to be wrought out, having been already partially developed, which will stand on yet firmer grounds of reason and demonstration than much of the boasted learning, which is now so often only an impediment to progress. Not in unkindness be it said to the votaries of old science, but with earnest desire to help them over the first stumbling-block of incredulity, "You are right in holding that nature's laws are not to be broken; but you are utterly wrong in assuming that there may not be laws of which you have no knowledge now, that suspend the action of the laws you do know." The words of an inspirational lecturer are apt in this connection. "Consider what your world has experienced in the intellectual development of mankind. Here in your atmosphere was held in reserve a power which you call electricity: for centuries it was unutilized, and you knew little of it: but now it is becoming one of your elements of power. In this element you have an illustration of the elements still beyond your conception, that have escaped your intellectual powers. It is unreasonable to suppose that you have exhausted nature's resources, or that in the future you will not discern many forces of which you now have no knowledge, which shall be applied to man's uses and for the benefit of the whole human race."

Interesting illustration of newly developing forces is found in the materialization of spirit forms and the accompanying phenomena, which those within the inner circles have watched with hope of further development, while outside observers are still contending, sometimes so bitterly, about the possibility of such manifestations ; unable yet to clear away their old stumbling-block of unbelief. The story briefly told eighteen hundred or more years ago, when the blessed powers of spiritual healing were refused their benign work " because of unbelief," so that he, the Master, " could do none of his wonderful works," is again repeated. Argument avails little to remove the obstacle. Nothing but the slow, hard logic of facts can overcome it, and gradually these facts are gathering with increasing potency. It is not that these facts are to be received without examination : no severer scrutiny has been instituted than by many who have outgrown their scepticism ;

but that they should be approached with willingness to receive when proved, no matter what points of old theology or accepted science may seem to be opposed. The old axioms of science are not contravened, but only the laws of external nature superseded, for the time, by the new forces of what for this purpose may be styled internal nature. Thus it has been demonstrated that Nature is all one, though the finer elements or forces are not cognizable to external observation, while they are everywhere underlying the ordinarily recognized material universe. Matter without — spirit within — and all in Nature, which includes the whole grand primary manifestation of the Supreme Being to man's comprehension.

The power to repel spirit manifestations, which is often unconsciously exercised by unwilling or incredulous minds, has been shown over and over again to observers of the phenomena. A marked illustration of this power was given at a materializing seance, in the difference between the writer's experience and that of a friend at his side, who could not refrain from continually questioning and doubting, though really desirous of attaining some convincing proof. At the

outset of these full form materializations a
cabinet has been necessarily used for the
purpose of isolating the medium, for the
time being, from the approach of unfavor-
able conditions, as well as for exclusion of
sunlight; the process of materialization, like
many of nature's processes, requiring seclu-
sion from light at the start. On the occasion to which we refer, the cabinet was a
small room, perhaps six by eight feet in dimensions, and satisfactorily closed against entrance or exit by any other than the one small
doorway, over which was hung a curtain.
The spirit forms taking visible and tangible
materiality from the elements of the physical body of the medium, who was reclining
in unconscious trance within the little room,
presented themselves at the small doorway,
drawing apart the curtains with their own
hands, and indicating by pointing as well as
by calling of names, the person from the
seance circle with whom they wished to communicate. Our friend was thus called up,
but to be disappointed in getting any satisfactory evidences of identity, either through the
face or form which were tangible, though in-
distinctly visible, or through any names given
or other words spoken. Very shortly after-

ward the writer was called to the curtained
doorway to be greeted by a figure taller than
the medium, and giving the name of a dear
relative who had passed to spirit life some
forty-five years before. The features were
plainly visible, and the lips substantial
enough to impress a veritable kiss. Upon
our inquiry whether another near relative was
present, who had passed away more recently,
the reply came distinctly, "Yes, wait a moment and I will bring her out to you." Retiring very briefly behind the curtain, the
figure again came forward, bringing the other
desired spirit, somewhat shorter in height,
with features not so distinctly visible, but
equally substantial in the greeting of love, accompanied by words of joy at the meeting.
While these two forms were standing thus
near, a third figure came out into the outer
room and moved about us, being recognized
by the conductor of the seance as one of the
"Cabinet Spirits," so called, who are in some
way accessory to the work of materialization,
especially when spirit friends manifest themselves in this way for the first time. Thus
there were three distinct spirit forms presented at one time; the first form melting
away before the second had finished the few

words of greeting: the whole appearance occupying some three or four minutes. Later on the same occasion the writer was called up to greet still another near relative, whose name was given, and who upon request taking his hand, came out to salute the assembled company, then retiring to the doorway of the cabinet dematerialized, sinking out of sight, as it were into the floor, and distinctly uttering the words " good-night " when half way down, and so finally disappearing at the floor as a light vapor !

At another seance of the same medium, a so called " Cabinet Spirit " came out into the outer room, plainly visible as a form, though with features a little indistinct, and taking the writer by the hand led him into the dark cabinet room for the purpose, as it proved, of satisfying him that the materialized figure was not the medium, but another and distinct spirit. Holding with his left hand to the hand of this spirit who remained standing at his side and visible in the dark by virtue of a phosphorescent light of its own, which seemed to permeate and radiate from the whole figure, the writer at the request of this cabinet spirit, with his right hand ascertained beyond question to his own mind, that

the medium was then recumbent in an arm
chair and in seeming unconscious state.
This experience was confirmed by others of
the seance circle taken in by the same spirit
form in the same manner. Similar experiences have attended, with many interesting
variations, the gradual development of this at
first very astounding phase of spirit manifestation.

Does the word " impossible " come to the
reader's mind, we can only say that these experiences were real to us, as similar proof has
been real to many, many seekers. Some fifty
years ago, when sitting with the then noted
medium, Daniel Hume, known afterwards as
D. D. Home, with two other near friends
about a table, and with all hands visible on
the table except our own, which were allowed
to be under the table, we had two well
formed hands placed in ours, one of adult
dimensions, and the other of infant size, and
both gently but distinctly grasped ; the first
being announced by the medium as of a near
departed relative, and the other as that of a
lost infant child. We knew it was no mere
imagination. It was but a question of time
and development from such beginning when
the full form materializations should become

possible, as they are to-day made manifest. By parity of reasoning the obscurities and difficulties still attending such manifestations must gradually disappear through better conditions of the witnesses in the seance chambers, and perhaps better understanding of the processes on the spirit side. Volumes could be filled with the veritable details already accumulated. That they are real is not matter of inference, but of knowledge on the part of those who have conducted their inquiries in the simplicity of a faith that is not hampered by too much learning of the old schools, or by mental prejudice that must ever be slow to find out new truth. The exposures which have been from time to time triumphantly announced, have in many cases been simply and only exposures of the ignorance and bigotry of the inquirers; for there is a *bigotry* of *unbelief* quite as rigid and unapproachable as the cast-iron beliefs of old theology. It must have set every thinking reader to very serious reflection to read, as he might in one of our prominent newspapers a few years ago, the account of such an exposure, with the earnest assurance that "any one who could still believe in such humbug must be a fool;" and to find in another col-

umn of the same journal the following item
under the head of cable news from London :
" Mysticism, Spiritualism, and the occult
sciences in any form are very popular just
now, not only in England, but throughout
the whole continent. It seems as if a wave
of thought were passing over Europe favor-
ing the supernatural. In fact mysticism is
becoming fashionable, and the last new
marvel is discussed in every drawing room
and at every dinner table." With so much
smoke, it may well be inferred that there
must be fire somewhere, and that it is spreading may be equally affirmed with such items
among the foreign cable news of the daily
press : a fire which the easy cry of " hum-
bug " will hardly put out, as it certainly has
not succeeded in doing yet, having rather in
most cases fanned the flame with the breath
that was meant to extinguish it.

One of the first objections raised by inquirers into these physical manifestations,
and perhaps their chief stumbling-block, has
been that the phenomena are, for the most
part, though not always, produced in comparative darkness. But it should be remembered that the want of light takes away
only one method of proof and identification,

namely that of sight; the other senses of
touch and hearing being still free to act,
while the evidence so obtained is confirmed
by proofs of intelligence and independent
action on the spirit side, quite precluding
the possibilities of automaton work. Besides, the difference between the self-luminous quality of the spirit form and that of the
medium in the dark cabinet or room before
described, was a veritable fact, and has been
noted by observers over and over again; a
fact of vision, and one which no one who
has experienced it would admit to be ocular
delusion, the vision being confirmed by the
contemporaneous testimony of the sense of
touch, the hand of the spirit form being distinctly held. In a general way the necessity
for exclusion of sunlight from the materializing seance rooms has been illustrated by
reference to other operations of nature,
which at their inception require concealment
and darkness as necessary conditions. Direct sunlight is, for instance too strong for
the ordinary germination of seeds, which
for the most part have to begin the process
of building up material elements about
their inherent spirit forms, under cover of
the soil, though that soil needs to be vivi-

fied sooner or later by the sun's rays falling upon it. In its incipient movement the life of the plant which is to be, or what may be termed its spirit, cannot bear the direct power of light. All animal life, including man, shows similar concealment to be necesary at its inception. Is not the ordinary process of developing photograph plates in a dark room another illustration of this common necessity? Perhaps this obstacle to belief may be lessened, if not wholly removed for some minds, by their considering what are the functions of sunlight in producing all natural phenomena. Is it not through the power of the sun's light that all forms once started into being are able to gather to themselves the elements which constitute their natural, visible composition and growth. We know how plants deprived of sunlight sicken and grow pale and feeble, if they do not die; seemingly unable to draw from the earth and atmosphere the elements which constitute their proper bulk. As the sunlight is thus essential to the aggregation of material elements into living forms, so it is powerful to hold together the elements when once thus incorporated. Deprived of its sustaining power those elements tend

sooner or later to feebleness of tension and
finally to disintegration. Now it appears
that the operation of materialization of spirit
forms is to disintegrate temporarily the elements, or portions of the elements constituting the physical form of the medium, and
appropriating these to the use of the materialized spirit form. Interesting experiments
have been reported in which the medium in
the cabinet was seated in a chair upon platform scales, so arranged that any change of
weight would be shown outside. When the
spirit forms appeared, it was testified that a
noticeable reduction of the avoirdupois
weight of the medium was indicated. The
operation must plainly be easier in the absence of the sunlight, the power which
originally was so important a factor in bringing those elements together in the body of
the medium, and helps to keep them there
in daily life.

On the other hand, the sudden introduction of light upon a materialized spirit must
operate to instantly send the denuded spirit
of the medium to resume possession of the
elements properly belonging to it, which had
been drawn away for the purpose of material
clothing to the spirit thus manifesting. Such

has been the experience in cases of exposure attempted in this manner by parties little understanding the conditions with which they were thus seriously and sometimes dangerously trifling, at the expense almost of the life of the medium. From all time the history of ghost seeing accords with this partial explanation. To make themselves visible to the natural eye or susceptible to touch, the spirits rising, as it has been generally termed, have of necessity borrowed temporarily of some form already materialized through the action of sunlight, and been able to retain the borrowed clothing only until the cock crow warned of the coming morning. By parity of reasoning it may be understood why a dim lamp light is more favorable to the manifestations than equally obscure day light; the lamp light being a reduced form of the original sun light, and so less powerful to resist the work of disintegration performed by spirits for their materializations.

Again it is matter of common observation with all inquirers that there is a force in the sun's rays more or less felt by everyone sensitive enough to permit the exercise of any form of mediumship, when the spirit influence draws near to control. Pain in the head and increased exhaustion are very commonly experienced by mediums when exposed to too strong light during the exercise of their peculiar vocation ; and this particularly at the beginning of their development. The sun light is too coarse or too strong for the finer conditions of spirit life ; the rays, which are themselves materialized forces, as it were striking too heavily upon the sensitive spirit, and causing the spirit, as well as the medium in sympathy, to shrink from its sudden or too powerful approach. If the mediums and their controlling spirits are thus sensitive, we can understand how the materialized spirits must be equally, if not more, quick to shrink from too strong light, and so find a reason for entire exclusion of light at the inception or taking on of the materialized form, and then for subdued light when they come out to be seen by the seance circle.

Another reason for the exclusion of sun light at these materialization seances is in the difference between the light which seems to belong to the spirit-spheres and that to which the natural eye is fitted. There is a wonderful luminosity of the spirit forms

varying in degree according to their conditions, and perhaps with the greater or less
refinement of the observer. This light pales
and disappears before the natural day, as
the stars of our evening skies do when the
morning comes, so that the spirits present
could not easily make themselves visible.
Such was the light before spoken of as ob-
served in the materialized spirit forms; a
peculiar transfusion of mild phosphorescence
making them appear self-luminous, which
would have been obscured by the stronger
rays of external sunlight. This light of the
spirit-spheres has been often testified to by
clairvoyant mediums as something beyond
the power of description.

To the further and not uncommon inquiry
of doubting minds, " Why do not the spirits
thus appearing give us some valuable information," one simple reply is, in the words
of another, " the mere fact of seeing or
sensing a departed spirit is of itself, great
information. Even a few raps from over
the river, telling us our departed friend is
alive, is information by the side of which
all other information pales." Indeed it is
the very stupendous character of these manifestations, these form materializations, when

first witnessed, which rouses all the forces of
unbelief so promptly, and makes the essential mental conditions of childlike receptivity
for the moment so difficult, and often so
impossible for the observer to retain. Instead of complaining that so little has been
gained in the developments of these forty
or fifty years, rather is there occasion for
wonder that such progress has been made in
so brief a period; and to accept the promises given that the way will yet open for
manifestations far beyond our hopes or im-
aginings. But in fact much information has
already been given through spirit sources,
to which we shall allude later.

It was said through the inspirational
speaker before quoted, " how unreasonable
are the old ideas of the spirit world, and how
at variance with all we know of nature and
what we, as spirits, bring to you! The di-
viding walls between you and the spirit world
exist in your own organisms, and they will be
annihilated. As the planet becomes purified, more attenuated and refined, your organisms will also be more refined, and you
shall, face to face, be in communion with the
inhabitants of the spirit world; for the time
cometh when clairvoyance will not be phe-

nomenal or exceptional as now, but when all
eyes shall be open to the realities of the world
in which dear ones are now dwelling."

With all these recognized phenomena of
materialization, which are accepted as facts
more or less by Spiritualists, it is nevertheless
to be candidly admitted that the last few
years have not shown that development in
this direction which the rapid opening of the
wonderful signs seemed at one time to indicate, and was indeed promised by the spirit
powers at work upon them. These manifestations have not progressed as hoped for and
expected, and it is matter of much questioning to know why. Two causes have been
suggested, both of which have doubtless been
largely instrumental in this slow advancement
amounting almost to stagnation. The first
of these is the failure of the seance circles to
recognize and so co-operate with the high
class of ancient spirits through whose labors
these full form materializations were at the
outset made possible. The conditions were
seized upon too often with mere selfish purpose of gain by the seance managers or con-
ductors ; the circles attending were actuated
by too mixed, if not low motives ; and the
mediums employed introduced elements of

greed instead of deep desire to help on the cause of truth, thus disappointing the high purpose of the ancient chemists, and opening the way to lower influences, which have been repellant, and checked the progress of development. The controlling relation of ancient spirits in this work then just opening, was declared emphatically by them in addresses made some fifteen years ago. The interference and assumption of other influences has caused the stay of progress which may not be renewed until these ancient bands are recognized and responded to by the more sincere and devout inquirers. A second probable cause of the delayed development may be found in the combined opposition to the work by old church influences, whose religious prejudice and bigotry have been potent to this end : ignorance of the truth and lust of power controlling and operating to mislead them all.

Among the many and varied instrumentalities employed in opening the way of life now more completely unfolding, these physical manifestations of spirit presence and power have their place ; but interesting as they are on the material plane, like many other spirit movements within and outside of old church

organizations, they are but means to the far
greater end of lifting humanity out of the
materiality of their conceptions of life, its
duties, its purposes and its occupations, into
more distinct perception of the spirit side of
being, which, with all the struggle and boasted
triumph over obstacles on the natural plane,
is the only reality to remain when the external
things are left behind. Come up higher, is
the call of the spirit. This does not mean
that the labors on the external plane are to
be given up; but that they be entered into
with far different and higher purpose than
now actuates the masses. " My Father
worketh hitherto, and I work," are the reported words of the Master; but filled with
what different motive from that shown in the
present prevailing scramble for the loaves and
fishes ! Not for self and personal gain or
aggrandizement, but for humanity is the call,
believing and seeking to realize the practical
meaning yet to be worked out in those often
quoted words, " Seek ye first the kingdom of
heaven, and all these things shall be added
unto you."

Those who consciously repel or are indifferent to these modern approaches of the
spirit-spheres, instead of welcoming the pos-

sible coming with patient inquiry, may know
thereby that they are hampered by prejudices
which are of mundane origin, and which
must ultimately give way to the increasing
light. It is not easy for those who have
experienced spiritual uplifting, and have perhaps attained high spiritual culture, to understand how they nevertheless may be and
often are closed by their mental states against
recognition of these modern approaches.
Deeming their illumination to be something
superior to the natural plane of experience,
as it is, they are prone to ignore the law
by which the light is permitted to reach
them as having universal bearing, and so are
unable to recognize the channels of communication through which often the spiritual
afflatus is breathed upon them. They can
reach by fine argument the principle of extension of what they recognize as natural
law into the spiritual world, but fail to perceive the possible reciprocity involved in the
spirit-spheres being permitted to respond
by direct approaches to the natural or external plane of human experience. This has
been illustrated through all the centuries,
from the time when sincerely devout Jews
ignored the presence of the Christ man who

had appeared among them from the obscure village of Nazareth, to these latter days when devout and spiritually uplifted Christ followers, in their turn, find no light in the developments of Modern Spiritualism. Assured through certain attainments and upliftings of the spirit, that they are not living on a low plane, many devout religionists of to-day refuse to be increased in their spiritual insight, as something they do not need, especially when it is offered through such sources as ordinary spirit mediumship. Can any good, they ask, come out of this new Nazareth? We would deal lovingly with minds so actuated, while drawing their attention, as in previous writings, to the calling of his disciples by the Master out of the ranks of simple-minded fishermen, rather than from the more cultured classes. The adaptation of those thus called was in their native sensitiveness and receptivity to things of the spirit, which do not come of mental training, but are in the nature of a gift. This has been shown in some simple-minded and uneducated public mediums of Modern Spiritualism, who while not developed mentally perhaps to be capable instruments for use by spirits of known attainments intellectually, may be and often are channels of spiritual communications of the highest order, though lacking the most cultured forms of expression. Those who content themselves with their spiritual attainments on the plane which they can in some sort intellectually understand and accept, may find themselves, when entering the spirit-spheres, easily superseded by many supposed inferior spirits who had been quite unknown to them in earth life. The story of Lazarus in Abraham's bosom illustrates a general truth beyond the compensation for lack of 'external riches. The heart which in its simple trust has been moved to spiritual uplifting in gratitude for a crust of bread, may be opened to a gift which might fail to come in response to the most solemn grace ever pronounced over a table loaded with external luxuries.

An interesting and to outside observers a confounding manifestation of spirit prompting and influence, has been the erection in Boston of the beautiful building known as " The First Spiritual Temple," as inscribed in scroll-work over the principal entrance. This building, raised largely by the accumulated means of one individual, whose motive in

the building and in its work since, has plainly
been most unselfish, however hampered and
obstructed by seen and unseen influences
opposed through ignorance and old church
prejudice, was dedicated to uses covering a
broad platform of philanthropies more or
less common to all associations seeking to
help humanity, with the one distinguishing
feature of continued spirit communion as a
basis of teaching and action, so that the
organization should not have its life closed in,
or its growth dwarfed by any form of eccle-
siastical rule, authority or dogma, which could
limit or restrain ever renewing and renewed
inspiration and revelation from the spirit-
spheres. From such sources alone are the
churches of to-day being brought to health
and higher usefulness, as indicated in the widening, liberal tendency of them all. In the
words of a recent inspirational speaker,
"The theologian is right when he says,
without a special revelation from heaven we
could know little of God and nothing of
immortality; he only gets wrong when he
limits that special revelation as God has
never limited it, and does not limit it."
With this broad fact held at the foundation
of all organizations, ever fresh recurrence may

be had to the sources of spiritual light,
which are waiting to send down their benig-
nant rays to man, as fast and as far as his
development will permit; and human progression will move on without hindrance, as
it is ultimately destined to do. Organization
is good in the greater power of combined
force for holding development already attained, and encouraging every effort to reach
up higher; but fatal to the ends of progress
when this power is used to close up the avenues of inspiration and revelation, for which
it can offer, as a poor substitute, only its
own self-constituted authority. This topic
has been markedly illustrated in the vain
endeavors at creed-bound organizations
among Spiritualists. It is a momentous
topic to the whole church of Christ to-day,
and indeed to every form of organization,
social, political or religious. Walls which
to-day may shut out evil, may to-morrow
prove barriers to the approach of good, and
in time need to be removed; and the mind
willing to act with God's will, must ever be
ready to aid in the removal.

We have claimed Spiritualism to be the
"Opening Way" to recognition and wise
reception of the philosophies of life which

are now unfolding to earth from the higher
spheres : philosophies not new in their fundamental ideas of love to God and man,
which are the essence of the Christ teachings
from all time, but in their practical ap-
plications of the brotherly love taught by
the Master, which are as yet so far from their
legitimate outworking for the good of all
men.   It is beginning to be accepted that
possession of wealth constitutes a stewardship for the benefit of many.   A further
stewardship is yet to be recognized in the
possession and use of brain force, whereby
those gifted with constructive powers of invention and organization, and possessing
quick insight into profitable results of labor,
will dedicate their powers more to the needs
and uses of their fellow men than to their
own selfish purposes and aggrandizement.
In every relation of life a call to come up
higher is sounding from the skies, to which
heed must be given by all who would find
themselves in any degree able to stand before
the judgment seat of these latter days.

ARTICLE VIII.

Spiritualism Waiting — Possession and Obsession.

Seeming to be at a standstill. — Motives of inquiry. — Difficulty of identification. — Testimony as to conditions in the spirit realms. — Wisdom of ancient spirits. — Progress retarded by antagonistic spirits and bands. — The Roman Church. — The freedom of Spiritualism opposed to all church rule. — The first Spiritual Temple again. — Lack of true seeking by inquirers a cause of outside indifference. — Spiritualists scattered through all the churches. — Spirit forces thus brought to bear. — Miracles old and new. — The Bible illuminated. — Objections considered. — Universality of mediumship. — Oliver Wendell Holmes. — Testimony of inspirational speakers. — Young inquirers to be restrained. — The home circle best. — Unbalanced mediumship. — Possession and Obsession, what are they ? — Insanity largely disorderly mediumship. — How to be treated. — Obsession in accordance with Law.

THE foregoing article has been directed mainly to a presentation of the more promi-

nent facts of spirit intercourse in the primary way of physical manifestations; and
has been gathered out of the writer's own
experience. It is admitted that progress in
this direction seems to have been stayed in
the past few years. The same is true of all
forms of spirit intercourse : and the question
is forced upon us, why has not Spiritualism
made greater advances, seeming sometimes
to retrograde rather than progress? Why
have not the avenues of mediumship in
general been opened wider — for clearer
identification : for more information regarding
the spirit-spheres; and for more light upon
all the strivings and trials of human life?
Is the fault in the votaries of Spiritualism;
or is the cause, though already so full of
wonders and helpfulness, to be laid aside and
gradually to pass out of view? We believe
the latter alternative to be impossible.

Inquiry into Spiritualism has been and
still is likely to be approached in three directions, each leading to collateral questions
and investigation according to the turn of
mind of the inquirer. The first and most
natural seeking is with desire to meet and
communicate with dear departed relatives
and friends, prompted by grieving hearts :

one word assured from that other side being
more effective to assuage the grief than all the
consolations offered from other sources. The
second desire, perhaps, is to become informed,
as far as may be, of the conditions of existence in the spirit realms; a natural inquiry in
that direction. The third and generally last,
is the willingness to be instructed through
advanced spirits who have attained greater
knowledge by long dwelling in the spirit-
spheres and it may be by many reincarna-
tions in earth life: and this independently
of names or personalities as affecting the
character of the highest teachings which the
inquirer can invite.

In the first line of inquiry one of the chief
difficulties has been the identification of spirits.
Messages may be received containing satisfactory test proof of the identity of a spirit announced; yet if the inquirer goes to another
medium seeking communication with the
same spirit, he may receive a different message
purporting to come from the same influence,
or he may be disappointed in getting any
response at all from the desired source. Exceptions to such experience have been happily
met and assured often enough to save the
discrediting of all communications; but the

general fact remains, without any comprehensive explanation other than is to be found in the mixed conditions of the spirit-spheres nearest to the earth plane. In that borderland we may easily believe, or rather would expect that there must be a conglomeration of influences well calculated to confuse the minds of spirits and the near friends seeking intercourse, and thus disturbing the conditions of the medium. Like the reflections of earth and sky shown on the surface of an unruffled lake, which become distorted by the first breeze that moves the quiet waters, so we can understand how mediums may be turned into uncertain and mixed communicators by the inharmonious conditions of the inquirers and of the spirits. There is much yet to be learned on both sides of the veil to make always sure that the loving messages are obtained as craved by a grieving heart on this side. It would seem the wisest course, for the present, if baffled in one direction, for the inquirer to try some other medium, until the one who evidently gives the best test and communication is found, and then to continue the seeking through such one.

In the second general direction of inquiry, —as to the conditions of life in the spirit-

spheres and their knowledge of mundane interests,—there has been much and very varied
testimony from the spirits according to their
standpoint, and doubtless also in a measure
to the wants of the inquirer's mind : for the
mental states of the seeker have much to do
with the shaping of responses. This need
not and does not lead to false statements,
but is likely to give emphasis in one direction
or another to special pictures of the spirit life,
which while true in their way and degree, do
not and necessarily cannot include in one
scene every phase of spirit existence. So too
in attempting to tell of coming events, which
spirits often see correctly in remarkable an-
ticipation, they are as often utterly in error
as to time, so that little reliance can be
placed upon such vaticination or benefit received, except possibly in putting the inquirer
upon his guard. Such effect may be quite as
well for the inquirer as if coming experience
had been laid out in reliable details of time and
circumstance ; and this for very obvious reasons, especially in the present whirlwind rush
of all human life. But there has been much
given, so far as the mortal mind can receive,
to show that the conditions in the spirit-
spheres are the prolongation or carrying out in

infinite variety, but unerring certainty, of the
tedencies of life which have been developed
in each individual through the mundane experience. This results in a judgment through
each individual soul, bringing joy to those
who by faithfulness to duty have earned the
salutation, "Well done, good and faithful
servant;" and to those who have failed to
improve their opportunities, every form of
retribution, down to the "lake of fire" and
the "wailing and gnashing of teeth;" figura-
tive but sometimes terrible sufferings that
must follow all wrong doing, through a
justice that cannot err.

In the third general direction of inquiry,—
the seeking of wisdom from advanced spirits,—quite as much has been given as the
mental states of the inquirers have been able
to receive and digest, that is make really
their own for guidance of conduct and better growth. These responses have in no
way improved upon the simple, fundamental
truths declared by the Master, so far as the
moral principles are involved; but they have
illustrated those principles with new light
which has often brought satisfaction and
growth of soul to the recipients. Obstacles
have been in the way to keep back such in-

struction, as in the other directions of inquiry, which may now be briefly considered.

Two forces seem to have been at work to
retard the progress hoped for at the first
recognition of possible communication with
the spirit-spheres : one arising from the opposition of spirit bands moved by various
motives to thwart Spiritualists in their desire
to know more, co-working with the antagonism of all the old church influences of those
still living on this side ; the second springing
from the failure of Spiritualists to recognize
that soul culture must underlie all their
seeking into spiritual things, if they would
see their cause grow in its proper potency,
and the ways opened to wider vision, and
deeper insight, into the wonders and mysteries of the life beyond.

The first of these opposing forces, the
intervention of antagonistic spirits, acting
individually and in bands, calls for careful
investigation and united action on the part
of truth-seeking Spiritualists. Prompted,
some of them, by merely mischievous desires, while others have doubtless been actuated by mistaken purpose to do God service,
these influences have continued a persistent
and more or less organized opposition. The

power of spirits banded together out of their habit of mind and fixed prejudices shaped through association with the various forms of church organization in their earth life, is only half realized by Spiritualists, and still less by those who have no knowledge of spirit return in these latter days. Of these forces, that of the Roman Catholic church, by its more complete organization, extended through so long time, has been the most active and persistent; and as in every contest moved by religious zeal, the most bitter of all the opponents; though the less concentrated opposition from those brought up in other forms of sectarian differences have taken their part in the contention. This power of the Roman church is not limited to those still in the earth form. Spirits who have gone over bound by their ideas of obedience to that mother church as their only surety for salvation, are naturally drawn together, and thus united have been and still are a power on the spirit side necessarily directed against all who do not accept the same authority on this side of life. Spiritualism demands and encourages a freedom of thought and inquiry into all things of the spirit, which no other organization has heretofore attained; and if that cannot be broken up and suppressed, the days of Roman supremacy, as well as the credal predominance of all other churches, are numbered. Recognizing this as the most threatening power which has yet been directed against the assumptions of Rome and its tributaries, these influences have sought to distract and cripple the labors and inquiries of Spiritualists in every way possible.

Such interference has been indicated in the history of the " First Spiritual Temple " in Boston, before referred to. Starting under auspices that seemed to promise the very best conditions for enlightening the community upon the highest phases of Modern Spiritualism, it was insidiously attacked by these old church forces, as seen at the time of its dedication by more than one clairvoyant medium, and so has been constrained in various ways from moving into the work laid out by its spirit founders and original promoters. Leading workers at its inception were removed by death or otherwise; one staunch man alone of them all, whose means chiefly had built the structure, they could not drive or persuade to give up his undertaking. They have succeeded in drawing away, temporarily as it would appear, many of its original supporters, and diverting them to other centres of spiritual communing and teaching; thus retarding the full uses into which the Temple will doubtless be ultimately brought, and toward which it appears to be now tending, though with small present encouragement. Should this seem improbable to have been so brought about, we would call to mind the long years of Roman Catholic rule, at one time controlling the whole civilized world, whose votaries passing out from earth life, must have been drawn together by the law of affinity which rules in spirit life, and continued their allegiance, with thought to serve God through advancing in every way the interests of the church below. Thus banded together in the spirit-spheres, they have been a mighty host through which the higher angels have had to struggle to let in the light which, notwithstanding the opposition, has given joy to so many minds. Such opposition to the Temple seems to have been anticipated in the higher councils which had its work in charge; so that they can and do accept it patiently, as in the ordering of a wise Providence, for purposes it may be of discipline and ultimate strengthening : and so the Temple and its work stand to-day a continuing surprise to outside observers, and to not a few of those who have attended its ministrations.[1]

Is there then no limit to this church power ? The free mind sees that it cannot be allowed to continue much longer its ob- struction to free thought, which shall lead every spirit, in or out of the body, directly to the Father of all spirit. The Roman Catholic church, so prominent in the exer- cise of such power, has grown, as we see it, like a huge tree from roots deeply imbed- ded in the earth plane, with St. Peter's as the central source of its life ; spreading its mani- fold branches over the mundane sphere and up into the nearest spirit realms. With all the beautiful lives, however, which have graced its rolls, and they have been many, though doubtless, out of their native quality, these would have been equally true and beautiful in their way, to whatever church they might have been attached, it is apparent to every outside observer that lust of power has grown to be its ruling motive, and by this it must ultimately perish.

[1] See Appendix.

For a purpose, doubtless, this growth of
power has been permitted : but with all its
seeming increase in some directions of late
years, it has reached its limit, as we see it, and
will ere long show signs of decadence and decay and cease to gather in new forces to per-
petuate its hitherto extended sway. We write
it not in unkindness, but in justice to truth
as it is shown to us. In God's good time
will developing humanity be left free to find
the good Father, and send its prayers and
thanksgivings up without waiting for church
or priesthood to cripple its natural, simple aspirations with ritual and form that kill the
spirit. Doubtless the Roman church and
all other creedal associations have filled, and
may yet fill a use in helping humanity up the
steeps of civilization ; and so far as they
have accomplished this, they are entitled to
recognition and gratitude ; but all the while
they have tended to keep their subjects in
swaddling clothes. Any church which ar-
rogates to itself the possession of all truth,
and claims through its head supreme control
of the spiritual interests of its people, with
infallibility in its decisions, must and will be
broken up, and ultimately merged in the
broader church of humanity. This broader

church will never presume to offer itself as
mediator between God and man, but only as
a loving helper to lift up the down trodden,
so long as there shall be such among Earth's
people, and to stimulate and guide human
aspirations to the highest source of Love and
Light they can reach.   The great tree of life
shall yet flourish.   With its roots imbedded
in the finer conditions of the earth sphere, it
will send forth leaves that shall be for the healing of the nations ; while its uplifting branches
shall pierce the spheres above.   It seems to
be law that the very highest spirit culture and
growth must have their beginning and foundation in the mundane state, constituting
thereby the wonderful circuit of life in which
all creation takes its part.   A recognition of
this law calls all the more to those still in the
earth sphere to do each their part in purifying
the soil for the opportunity of the great Tree's
roots, down to the subtlest filament of its
basic growth and expansion.   Thus the millennial days will come with rejoicing not only
to those yet in mortal form, but send their
joy up to the outermost or innermost spheres
encircling this regenerated planet.

The second prominent cause of the seemingly slow progress of Spiritualism during

later years, has been, as before noted, in the
failure of Spiritualists to recognize that soul
culture must underlie all their seeking into
spiritual things, if they would see these things
expand into wider and more beautiful development. Want of this has been noticed by
outside observers, who seeing the comparatively external interest of many Spiritualists
in the mere phenomena, have been deterred
thereby from any serious investigation. The
prevailing dormant interest in things of the
spirit has received slight awakening from the
mere curiosity seeking in Spiritualism. Such
seeking has little power to break up the intellectual unbelief which has grown to such
proportions, led on by the universal drift of
intellectual activity in the development of
material interests, till utterly absorbed and
spell-bound in the greed for money making
and grasping; now the dominant force
throughout the civilized world. Beautiful
exceptions to this drift are to be found, and
we must hope that they will prove to be a
leaven to leaven the whole lump in coming
time; but they are exceptions rather than the
rule; and even they can hardly free themselves
from the influences of their environment
which have so completely crushed out all

power of discerning spirits and spiritual things recorded as possible and actual attainment in the olden time.

Meanwhile there has been in recent years a growing freedom of the old churches toward independent inquiry of the individual mind, tending to send old theologies into the back ground. This process is going on with rapid strides. Men and women are asking not so much what the true interpretation and meaning of the old theological confusions may be; but rather how they can rise to a higher, purer plane of culture in all the ways and doings of their daily lives. In sympathy with this feeling many Spiritualists who have recognized the want of the highest interest in the public gatherings of the believers, are to be often found now attending the meetings of the more recently liberated disciples of the Christian fold, rejoicing to hear the direct application of the Christ teachings. Bringing with them their conviction of the presence of denizens of the spirit-spheres, they open the way, through their unspoken belief, to nearer approach of the higher bands, who have been pressing in upon earth life since the advent of Modern Spiritualism to help humanity to something more than mere expression of acceptance of the Christ principles. Such infiltration of spirit influence among the more liberal and growing churches cannot fail to be adding its part in the general awakening, so that it would be no matter of surprise to see very striking manifestations of spirit presence break out in the very midst of some of the oldest church organizations, such as may for a time quite surpass in beauty and power the best that have yet been shown in gatherings of recognized Spiritualists.

It is not easy to appreciate, though it has often been stated from various spirit sources, through what a dense stratum of lower influences these higher bands have had to find their way in their approaches to earth life — the many, many souls that have passed out of their mundane existence in undeveloped conditions, and so are held spell bound by mundane attractions. Spiritualists who have opened their minds and hearts too unreservedly to the approaches of these lower spirits have found, often to their cost, that not every influence that may come is to be trusted, though they may present themselves under the guise of angels of light; learning by experience that the "gates ajar"

are opening equally to all the spirit-spheres
attached to this planet. Try the spirits was
the Apostle's injunction. It has been and
still is a yet more needed warning in these
latter days of closing in of the old and opening of a new era for humanity. That bands
of advanced spirits, though not recognized
by all, have actuated the minds and teachings of the free souls who in very recent
years and with increasing power have come
out from the limitations of old theology, and
are now feeding the hungry crowd so long
unsatisfied and restless with the husks that
have been offered them before, is believed
by the enlightened Spiritualists who have
been rendering good service through their
unspoken influence and their desire to har-
monize with the outworkings of the new
freedom. By experience they know the
value of their conviction of the near presence of the spirit-spheres ; how it has given
a reality in their consciousness to all things
of the spirit, which they could not attain
before, until freed from the shackles thrown
over their minds by the wide-spread, absorbing interests on the material side of life.
The wonderful development of external science and art; the overcoming of so many

impediments on the natural plane by inventions ; and the consequent selfish struggles of competition in every direction, have in the century now drawing to its close so blinded the seekers who have followed in the old lines of spiritual inquiry, that they have been for the most part but groping after truth.

An evidence of this blindness has been shown in the disposition to deny the so-called miracles of the early Christian centuries, repetition of which in these latter days, through the labors and sufferings often of spirit mediums, has thrown so much light upon those old recorded experiences, and opened the way to a better understanding and acceptance of the ancient scriptures. With this help the Bible has been read under a new light ; and all the teachings of the wonderful Book have been received with a new power, notwithstanding the disposition of some Spiritualists to throw it aside, when they first began to realize how creed-bound they had been under their former reading and teachings. Albeit that the new light came to their minds through physical manifestations, the tiny raps it may have been, giving intelligent response from that hitherto unknown side of life, they have at first yielded to the pendulum swing and gone over some-

times to violent negation of their previous
beliefs. Gradually attaining a better understanding of spiritual things, they have become
settled to an equilibrium nearer the truth,
and so ready to rejoice, with a new satisfaction, in all the good that has been and is to
be gained out of all Scriptures of the past.
May it not be that the religious world is
waiting now unconsciously for a revival such
as has not been known in this day and generation, springing out of the minds cleared
largely, though indirectly, through Modern
Spiritualism, which whether recognized or
not, has quickened and helped on their growing freedom and more direct aspirations.
Spirit mediums will not cease to be developed
and help the work on; but they will be on a
higher plane of seeking, and draw more advanced bands from the spheres to join in the
redemption of man on lines so plainly shown
by the Master eighteen hundred or more years
ago, and still so far from being directly applied
to the practical issues of every day human experience. Then altruism will cease to be
something talked of as a sort of new philosophy, but in very truth the outworking
of the Christ teachings ; and lead to what
will be indeed a new heaven and a new earth,

for the peace and rejoicing of every well born child of man.

It may be helpful here to meet and we hope throw light upon some of the obstacles to acceptance of Spiritualism, which have been encountered by too hasty or prejudiced inquirers. An early objection offered has been that "Spiritualism is only one theory among various possible explanations of the phenomena." The error lies in not recognizing the fact that while other theories may account for some and perhaps many of the phenomena, the Spiritualist theory is the only one that can meet all the facts. The closer that scientists examine into the mysteries, the more they are forced to this conclusion, however unwilling they may be to accept it as the only way out of the dilemma into which the many and varied manifestations have forced them. Again, "dependence upon physical proof for the hope of immortality," is complained of. The necessity, and it has been and still is to outside observers a necessity, that the inquirer "must play the part of a detective; must guard against frauds; must invent ingenious tests; must be ready to work in the dark," comes, as has been said over and over again, from the mental state of the community at large, which has lost the power of discerning spirits, recognized as once possible in the early days of the Christian dispensation ; so that physical proofs and the necessarily accompanying methods of testing them, have been the only possible avenue of approach on the spirit side. The difficulty is complicated by the fact that the state of mind in which the inquirer approaches his investigation has often much to do with the character of the manifestations, in whatever way they may be presented. So sensitive are the conditions of mediumship that suspicion of fraud in the mind of the inquirer invites the very fraud he would repudiate, and opens the way to the approach of false influences, which rejoice in every opportunity to deceive. For best results the inquiry must be conducted with minds clear of preconceived ideas and prejudices, and so be able in child-like receptivity, not childish credulity, to recognize and measure true conditions fairly presented. Like the mariner's compass, these conditions are sensitive to the approach of any opposing or diverting influence, and while pointing to truth when not interfered with, they can be and too often are deflected, and so made to appear false and unstable.

Another objection raised, that " no important communication of any great human invention or discovery, and no new thought, or a line of great poetry, have been given through mediums," shows the mistaken ideas held by many people concerning mediumship. Spirits from the spheres about us, individually or in bands, encompass every human being while in mortal form, and have more or less to do with the shaping of each life. Most students of the subject have been persuaded of this. Now, while every one is thus more or less mediumistic, that is moved upon, prompted, and guided by influences from the spirit-spheres, divinely appointed agencies, according much with and attracted by the character of each individual, the publicly recognized mediums are those who not only are prompted in the conduct of their own lives more or less consciously, but can be used to give communications to others. When so used as channels for communication, much may depend upon their average development as fit instruments for the varying powers of the spirits communicating. Under such often inferior instrumentalities highly developed spirits could hardly be expected to equal their utterances when in the mortal form ; nor be able to communicate any great inventions or discoveries through brains totally unfit for such use. Added to this impediment is the possibility that the name given with any communication may be wholly assumed, and the communication come from some inferior spirit, willing to trifle with the eagerness of the inquirer. Recognizing the fact of more or less universal mediumship, in varying degrees of development, it may be understood that all inventions are, more or less, given by impression to waiting minds ; coming we know not from how high source in aid of those seeking in the direction of discovery ; and more or less owing to the sensitive or mediumistic character of the individual so touched or prompted. The words of the old fable are applicable here, as in so many other ways of human effort and development : " Put thy shoulder to the wheel and then call on Jupiter, and he will help thee." They are, in a way, applicable to all mental action, which is more or less inspired by and mingled with impressions thrown upon the receptive brain from invisible sources ; it may be from spirits, or perhaps from the great reservoir of knowledge that seems to envelop and quicken all life on the planet and the spirit-spheres connected with it. This does not interfere with, but flows into and develops each one so impressed, resulting in a culture of the mind, and through that an awakening and growth of soul powers, which is the ultimate end of all human endeavor and experience. Many a man has prided himself as the originator of fine thoughts and creative inventions, which came to him rather from inspiration : the new idea often springing into his consciousness at some unexpected moment; perhaps after being baffled by ineffectual efforts to seek the desired end through his own independent thinking and efforts. Over and over again has this been shown in human experience. A well-known author and poet expressed himself a few years since as follows :[1] " I wrote the poem rather as a duty than as a pleasure ; and yet here and there I found myself taken off my feet by that sudden influx of a tide that comes from we know not whence, but which makes being, and especially in-

[1] Oliver Wendell Holmes to his friend, John G. Whittier.

ternal vision, so intense and real. You, as a poet, know so well what that means." . . . " I think that some of the most real moments of life are those in which we are seized upon by that higher power, which takes the rudder out of the hands of *will*, as the pilot takes the place of the captain in entering some strange harbor; and I am sure I never know where I am going to be landed from the moment I find myself in the strange hands of the unknown power that has taken control of me." What is this but mediumship, when the brain so touched had, by its own development or natural gift, reached a stage which could be receptive to such impulse and impression from spirit sources, and the occasion invited such use?

Similar testimony, though from a different point of view, comes from the statement of inspirational speakers, some of whom are conscious of standing outside their bodies and listening to the words uttered through their own lips but by other controlling speakers, and which on their returning to self control could thus be remembered, and in some measure repeated; while other speakers are entirely unconscious when so used, and of course have no memory of

what has been said. As before stated, the
name given by the spirit communicating may
be assumed ; to satisfactorily determine which
might require much scrutiny and experiment.
This seeming difficulty has its good results
in leading to the conclusion, that all that
comes from the lips of spirit mediums should
be judged by its own elements of truth, as
recognized by the inquirer, rather than taken
on the authority of the name given ; while
by no means precluding the possibility of
the name given being really that of the spirit
prompting to speak or write. Is there then
no value, it will perhaps be asked, in the words
or writings of one who has proved himself a
wise counsellor and friend to humanity by
past good works and teachings, which have
earned for him a name to be trusted? Certainly there is, and in the ordinary course of
life such authority is to be relied upon until
something better is shown ; but the fact
remains that the listener or reader really
appropriates only so much as he can receive,
and so far only gains by it ; just as in matters of pure science he holds any new truth
only until some other dictum has been
proved to be the more correct and advanced.
Soul growth, like every other growth, is

attained by accretion of new life, new thought, new power, adding their mite each day to the process of advancement; while stagnation, which is the other alternative, may lead down to decay and dissolution. In offering this explanation, however, we would not be understood to admit that little or no new truth has been brought by the higher bands through recognized mediumship, to the comprehension and aid of truth seekers. Much has been given, and much more will be, as conditions favor and minds are receptive.

The possibility of misleading mediumship through control of mischievous spirits has been suggested; and it has been asked, "Shall we not then decry all open gifts in this direction as dangerous" and "fear to have our children interested in this strange and misty borderland?" Doubtless there is need of caution in inviting the young and inexperienced to go into the inquiry through any and every public medium who may be found. As with every other gift there must be some prudence exercised in our use of this of mediumship, or it may prove a stumbling-block and mischievous; especially in these days of confusion at large, and still incomplete knowledge of much that is comprehended under the name of Spiritualism. If the young are brought into opportunity to observe the phenomena, it should be in company with older and experienced inquirers who are sincere seekers, making the two or three gathered together in the name of truth. Rarely, if ever, should mediumistic qualities when indicated in any young person be encouraged to their full expression, until the years of maturity in body and mind are reached. Too early giving up to such use, if quickened beyond simple growth, may prove exhausting to both body and mind, and perhaps prevent what might otherwise, in later years, prove a healthy, well-balanced and beautiful mediumship. The use of any instrument such as the " talking-board," so-called, is especially to be avoided for children. These may or may not give true response ; the character of the communications through them depending so much upon the mental states of the inquirer, whether young or mature. Their very form is calculated to divert the mind from serious investigation into mere idle questioning, and so inviting a low class of spirits to raise false hopes and otherwise mislead the childish mind. If used in the hands of a child alone, these modes of seeking give too easy play to the idle fancies of their solitary devotees.

It would seem that the highest and best mediumship is cultivated by retiring into one's self in silence, and then prayerfully opening the doors of the soul to such impressions and such growth as one can be capable of attaining through earnest desire to seek only truth ; and this without neglecting, but rather with the more zeal fulfilling every external duty to which there may be plainly a call. Not infrequently such fulfilment of external duty has proved the best opportunity for the unfoldment desired. When, however, several like-minded persons gather in circle for the common good, their united, prayerful seeking may draw down much blessing of the spirit not otherwise to be reached. Thus it is desirable, when possible, to have in every home, as before written, some resting-place, some holy of holies, where the members of the family may gather, however briefly, to invite such blessing as may be most needed for each member. Few words suffice at such times to help concentrate the minds of those present upon the purpose of their gathering, and the loving messengers of God will do the rest in beautiful uplifting and strengthening for good, which is of God. The home so conducted and blessed will ever prove a place of refuge to all its members who, no matter how far separated, will return in spirit to its loving embrace, until all may perhaps in time form new home circles of their own. Such life from generation to generation would do much toward realizing the promised millennial days, and throw back the bars that could no longer keep man out of his paradise regained.

In this broad view of mediumship it will be seen that it is not true that "mediums are generally in unbalanced nervous equilibrium and live close to the danger line of insanity," as has been charged; though doubtless some are so conditioned. The question has often been mooted, "Is genius allied to insanity?" Undoubtedly it is, since genius is another word for the very receptivity of mind to spirit impression and influence, such as characterizes the more avowed and public cases of mediumship. Thus it may and does sometimes happen that men of so-called genius are in "unbalanced nervous equilibrium," and sometimes, it may be only temporarily, do topple over the "danger line of insanity." But such instances are hardly to be held up as warnings against the possession and use of powers which are ordinarily recognized as belonging to genius.

This brings us to a deeply important and sadly interesting direction of inquiry into Modern Spiritualism, in its bearing upon the question of insanity, as ordinarily understood; and the light it throws upon the proper treatment of victims of 'that malady, as indicated in what are recognized as orderly and disorderly mediumship; the former being known as "possession," where the spirit control is temporary and under the direction of some guardian spirit or band; and the latter as "obsession," when the medium's proper self is so merged or held by spirit influences, that it cannot ward off their approaches, or get relief from their more or less continuous control, and is unable, to that extent, to assert or express its own individuality. This latter condition is ordinarily recognized as insanity, and practically it is such, and often most sadly. There may be no discoverable disease or lesion of the brain, and yet the symptoms show the lack of self-control constituting insanity.

Spirits of varying degrees of development are more or less about every individual in mortal form; being by no means limited to recognized mediums; their character depending largely upon the conditions of each individual. Every inquirer soon learns that in all orderly mediumship some other Intelligence than the medium's self does, for the time being actuate, and more or less completely control the mental action, whatever the nature of the communication thus given; the experience being of the same general character, whether high or low influences are permitted to manifest their presence. The control passes off after its communication has been given; its mission so far filled; and upon its leaving, the medium's own spirit resumes its proper control. This simple statement has been substantiated by too many thousand inquirers to be questioned now, however unwilling the minds of outside observers may be to accept it. But strange and perhaps low spirits may and do break in, sometimes it would appear quite unawares to themselves, and get more or less control of any man or woman whose proper self-control has been lessened or lost through conditions of mere physical health, it may be; or more com-

monly through severe trials of experience
that have exhausted the natural healthy
forces of the mind; thus excluding or shutting in the proper master or mistress of the
house, and making a disorderly mediumship
or obsession. In orderly mediumship the
extent to which such undeveloped spirits
may use the medium if allowed to control,
is held more or less under the direction of
the guardian spirit or band presiding over
the manifestation; such protection or guardianship being a well recognized fact among
Spiritualists. In disorderly mediumship,
commonly looked upon as insanity, such
protection seems to be more or less sus-
pended under the repelling force of the conditions involved, and the manifestations of
spirit presence and control are full of vagaries,
and not infrequently accompanied with violent demonstrations quite foreign to the
natural characteristics of the patient's proper
self, and very difficult to manage or understand. When such cases have become deep
seated and long continued, nothing short of
the Christ power can reach them to cast out
the control at once; while the unbroken
perseverance and never failing love of an
attendant in charge can perhaps gradually lift

the obsessing spirits so that they will leave before they have worn out the body in which they have themselves become, as it were, incarcerated, and the patient's own spirit may by degrees, through similar loving care and encouragement, be strengthened to resume its proper control.

Painful opportunity for study in this direction has been given the writer; and over and over again with most convincing demonstration of spirit obsession; the patient, having lost control of self, and being more or less continuously under some so-called hallucination. Had the conditions of obsession been better understood at the outset of this case, long years of watching and waiting might perhaps have been shortened. But by way of compensation, it has been stated from the spirit side, that no one can measure the amount of good that may be accomplished, under rightly directed care and treatment, for obsessing influences who are thus brought within reach of light for which they may have been long groping in utter darkness and despair; a good declared to be more than recompense for the labor and sufferings of the obsessed patient and watching friends! As "from seeming evil still deducing good," God ever makes the wrath of man to praise Him, so in the orderings of his providence may the insane patients be instruments for good, at which ultimately they may rejoice, notwithstanding the suffering caused. We cannot and do not know all that is yet to be learned in such cases; but enough has been shown to give a new and deeply interesting aspect to this most distressing form of human experience.

With all the liability to spirit influence and control shown in this article, we would repeat the injunction before written, calling upon every one to see to it that their lives are ordered with ever watchful purpose to "resist every prompting or impulse that is not in accord with their highest sense of right." Individual responsibility to this end is still man's first obligation to himself and to God, as it is his special prerogative and glory in the struggles and attainments of his daily life.

Conditions often very difficult to understand and wisely help occur more frequently than generally recognized, when obsessing spirits have made partial approach toward control of their subjects, but not enough to take away all responsibility of action. The state which follows is very trying to friends who cannot but see the unbalanced mind, yet find it difficult, often impossible, to persuade the subject to yield to any reason, or to realize that he is " beside himself." Persons so affected are looked upon as " very odd," sometimes annunciating the most unreasonable propositions, and doing the most unreasonable things, while yet retaining enough of self to save them from guardianship ; though they may be most uncomfortable and difficult inmates of a household. These conditions may continue for years under the suffering patience of relatives and friends, or they may deepen into states absolutely demanding outside control ; or happily, by entire change of surroundings and interests may be, and not unfrequently are, entirely thrown off. Such cases are distinctly allied to recognized mediumship and obsession, and can be understood from no other point of view. Similar conditions may and doubtless do obtain more or less in the delirium of fevers ; the manifestations in which have so long been waiting for explanation from current medical science.

It is true that careful observation has

shown to those who have devoted themselves to treatment of the insane, that a most
important end to be labored for is to
strengthen the individuals affected, so that
they can command and use their own proper
mental action. So far, so good. But they
have not attained the deep yet simple understanding which will show to the careful,
loving attendant the absolute necessity of
most patient speech and action toward the
obsessing influences, and how by kindness
and instruction to lift them gradually to a
higher plane of thought and character, until,
as sometimes occurs in a way not yet fully
understood, nature opens the doors, perhaps
suddenly after long years of obsession, for
their departure, so that they can no longer
hold sway ; or until of their own accord they
yield to the loving pressure of those laboring
to restore the patient. Both the patient and
the obsessing spirits need help ; and very
interesting and encouraging will such management be found by those called to such
cases ; it being borne in mind that careful
and repeated observation only, and this not
always, will help to determine the identity
of the infesting spirits, and so aid in their
further instruction.

Among other efforts at ameliorating the condition of the insane, recent experiments in hypnotic treatment, an old force under a new name, now beginning to be recognized by official science as offering invaluable healing power when rightly used, seem to indicate that it may become of special use in the care and cure of insane patients. We would urge such operators to study and understand spirit obsession, so that in their treatment the hypnotic suggestion may be thrown upon the obsessing spirit or spirits, as well as upon the patient. If that can be accomplished, it must help to important progress in this branch of medical science.

Again, knowledge of the possibility of spirit obsession would help all who by temperament or otherwise are too easily brought to extreme expression of emotion, to beware of the danger in giving way to their impulses of anger, or grief, or even of joy, however short their yielding may be in duration. Every instance of this want of self-possession gives opportunity for spirit influx, which by too great continuance or frequency may become supreme, and in the end wreck the happiness, if not the life of the sufferer.

That there are cases of insanity attributa-

ble directly and wholly to physical injury or
disease, the removal of which will restore the
lost equilibrium, constituting sane health, is
not to be questioned ; but in such cases there
is opportunity for inroad from wandering
spirits to complicate, and make treatment
more difficult and slow of results. Such
cases do not contradict our general position,
and may, in their way, confirm it ; calling
often, in the course of their procedure, for
careful study and understanding of the phenomena of Modern Spiritualism

In every direction and form of life it is
the law that true health depends upon main-
tenance of the equilibrium, which belongs to
the component elements of every living form.
Any loss of such equilibrium opens the way
to invasion from opposing forces, which will
attach themselves to the failing part, and if
not driven off, may in the end ruin the
blighted form. This is simply true throughout all organic life, and plainly manifested
in every injury that reaches the vegetable or
animal form. Parasites numberless are
ready to ingraft themselves into every
wound of the plant or animal. The possibility of spirit obsession is one form of such
parasitic life affecting human beings ! When

one considers the myriads of spirits in human form who have passed out of their earth bodies in the lowest conditions of development into some sort of spirit existence, and thus earth-bound must be slow to rise above the earth plane, it seems a cause for wonder that any human life can be protected from possible inroad. Only in health of body and mind is such protection to be found. It must be by virtue of the slow but higher development of succeeding generations, and stronger hold upon the principles of true life, though yet far from being fully attained, as well as by the watchful help of the higher influences of the spirit-spheres, who under the good Father's care and prompting are more than able to cope with these lower destructive forces, that humanity has continued to exist upon the earth, and is gradually developing into higher expression upon that plane ! Such view of the situation calls all the more to each and all, by true living, to do their part in the lifting of the race.

See Appendix.

ARTICLE IX.

CLOSING ILLUSTRATION. — SOUL CULTURE
THE CHIEF END OF SPIRITUAL SEEKING.
— THE MARRIAGE RELATION IN
CONCLUSION.

A judgment upon neglected opportunity given in
illustration. — Soul culture. — The marriage relation. — Its high calling. — The divine right
and duty of woman. — Man to be restrained
while sharing the responsibilities of parentage.
— True freedom in love not selfish. — The lower
promptings to be subservient to spiritual control.
— A crime against humanity. — False needs
from selfish beginnings. — Magnetic interchange
appointed. — Intemperate indulgence in food
leads to disobedience of Law. — A spirit communication upon marriage. — Free love, what is
it? — Apostrophe to truth. — Unveiling of Truth
essential, where ignorance is not bliss. — An inspirational view of what "this orb is yet to be."
— The writer's early compassion and prompting. — True Motherhood the crown of Womanhood.

THE story has been told of one of our
real estate magnates, who had passed into

spirit life a few years ago, while in possession of house upon house, and in receipt of
thousands in rentals, that upon being asked
by a friend, through a spirit medium, " what
he had been doing during the year which
had elapsed since his departure," the spirit
replied — " Doing? I have been trying to
find bricks enough to build a house with ! "
He had been so absorbed in his material
interests, and had availed so little of his
opportunities to help others out of his
abundant wealth, that he had utterly failed
to put together the elements of righteous
living wherewith to build the house " not
made with hands," which he might otherwise have found ready to welcome him on
that other side ; — and there he stood before
the questioner, houseless and homeless !
Such announcement must have been sadly
instructive to the inquiring friend, as to
every thinking mind. The incident is introduced here in part for its general illustration
of the many and varied teachings which have
come through Modern Spiritualism ; but
more as a call to all who are looking into
modern things of the spirit, to come up
higher, and to remember that true spiritual
unfoldment should be the chief end of all

the inquiry ; failure in which has been stated
to be the second prominent cause of the slow
progress in Spiritualism during recent years.
Too many Spiritualists are sticking in the
beautiful gates, instead of entering into the
inner precincts of the Temple, to learn and
to worship, and ultimately to unfold in loving service to humanity !

Soul culture—what is it, and how to be
attained ? First and foremost it is to be
reached through faithful performance of
every duty in external life to which we may
be called, without other thought than its
proper fulfilment. While not neglectful of
self, so far as care may be needed to keep
each life in its best condition for usefulness,
growth of the soul seems to come more out
of work well done for other use and purpose
than from direct seeking for its own development. It is altruistic in the fullest sense.
The powers which may be developed through
soul culture are matters of growth, up to the
almost limitless expression of what lies more
or less dormant in every human being; and
they are to be dedicated to the highest uses
of which each individual may be capable.
It was said recently by an earnest truth-
seeker, that her spirit seemed " like a young

robin with upturned head and open mouth,
waiting for the inflowing of truth." So we
would wish that every soul should hold itself
ready to welcome and use for the help of
others, as well as of itself, every thought that
has real life in it, every truth wherewith the
good Father is ready and waiting to satisfy
and bless his hungering children. This is
no new need peculiar to Spiritualists; it has
been the cry of all leaders in spiritual things.
But it is to be pressed with special force on
those whose minds have been awakened to
the latter day possibilities of development
through more intimate relations with the
spirit-spheres, that they may show by their
fruits what growth and blessing are to be
gained by deeper insight into this opening
way of life.

In response to the call to come up higher,
which seems to have been in the air during
the last quarter century, with all the greed
and rush for money making, many minds in
and out of the churches of to-day have
been and are busy with plans for ameliorating the conditions of the less favored children of men, and lifting them to a plane
which shall be more worthy of the Christ
name, now sadly a misnomer in so many

directions of our boasted progress and refinement ; and to these all we would heartily wish
a God-speed. Our own thought turns, in
such connection, to what we have previously
but briefly adverted to, as the most momentous of all questions pressing to-day, and
indeed through all time, upon the need of
mankind ; we mean the near relations between man and woman. Due consideration,
or rather study of this grave question is still
held strangely in the background, while the
nations go rushing on in their pursuit of
wealth and all external gratification ! With
spillings of their mad gains they are building
hospitals, asylums, and jails for the sick, the
insane, and the criminal, to meet the consequences of ignorance and too wilful neglect
of the basic prevention of all sickness and
crime to be assured through a better understanding and ordering of the marriage relation, and the holy duties of parentage !

With fear and trembling we approach this
momentous subject, so plainly to our mind it
is the first and last great need to be rightly
studied and understood. In the solution of
the questions involved in it, as it seems to us,
lie the ultimate uplifting and perfection of
the human family. Too long have the mass

of mankind closed their minds against a righteous study and wise unfoldment of the deep mysteries which have been implanted through nature in the wonderful structure of the bodies of man and woman in special regard to continuation and development of the race. Hedged about by attractions of sense, which lead to healthful interchange when wisely exercised, but to degradation and ruin when indulged in only for selfish gratification, the marriage relation has been subjected to every trial possible in the wide range of human error. Beginning with the lowest forms of its expression among the earlier and often inferior races, and developing through the centuries up to the present bounds and limitations which society has slowly worked out for its own protection, the restraints do help to keep the selfish instincts in subjection to the law of social order. But this is comparatively external in operation. Man must yet find his way out of the wilds in which his labors first opened, to the fairer fields that are awaiting him, when his spiritual nature has attained the predominant relation to his life, prefigured in the paradisiacal state; — the paradise lost, but yet to be regained.

The question of love, as distinguished

from attraction on the lower or physical
plane, demands a deep study for most of
the present generation of men and women,
whose antecedents and inheritance have been
out of such mixed conditions as often to
confuse the most earnest investigator as to
the real source of the promptings ordinarily
attributed to love. The first claim of Spiritualism in this regard has been for freedom, as
we have before written, from the tyrannical
control of man over woman, which has been
handed down through many centuries, and
sustained with slowly yielding provisions by
statutes of man's making. If not demanded
as a brutal right, the result has been too
much the same through woman's fear that
failure to meet his selfish importunity may
turn him away from his proper home, and
so with trembling as to possible results, she
has yielded herself against the finer instincts
of her nature! What a breach of divine
law is involved in this sacrifice on her part,
and what a lowering of true manly attributes
on his part. On the other hand, artificial or
any other unnatural interference in the intercourse, is but a disgrace to humanity, and
will sometime, if not always now, be recognized by every true man and woman as un-

worthy of the high calling of a child of God.

Every branch of the Christian church has taken its part in endeavoring to keep sensual license within bounds. Some portions of it have held that marriage can be rightly consummated only under its ordinances; almost ignoring the divine law which first moves the twain to be joined as one, and which if rightly studied and obeyed would, and in God's time will determine the character and holiness of the joining, as no priest or earthly potentate ever has or could. To be a law unto themselves, so that statute law with penalties attached, as well as solemn injunctions of the church, and promises at the marriage altar shall cease to be necessary restraints, is plainly the divine end to be attained; just as all laws become useless when the community over which they stand as sentinels and guards have risen above the possible need of such protection. This is easily written, but to be accomplished requires a devout study, on the part of every man and woman coming to maturity, to know themselves physically and spiritually, before entering into the sacred relation of marriage; realizing that with or without church and state they are children of God through whom they have their being, and that in his service, not in their own selfish seeking, the consummation is to be reached.

Among the various effects produced upon the public mind through the advent of modern Spiritualism, tending in all directions to freedom of thought and action, and so seeming to loosen old restraints, the license in which some of the early votaries of the new truths indulged their lower natures, has at times cast a shadow upon the real purpose and message of the angel visitors. Like many truths when first broached upon the consciousness of men, this freedom has proved a stumbling-block, partly because misunderstood, and partly because, as before written, the old conditions could not bear the nearer approach of the sun of righteousness, the very principle of unselfish love, and so quickened they have smouldered and smoked, and at times burst into flames that must be restrained and extinguished by external law.

Many pages have been written and published by earnest seekers after truth in this direction, and none more exhaustive of the question of freedom in love than the controversy between two able disputants published a few years since.[1] But the arguments seem to fail of definite conclusions in not striking deep enough into consideration of the divine purposes involved in marriage ; and the principle of freedom is still waiting to be apprehended and demonstrated in the expression of a truer, less selfish, and more spiritual love between man and woman than is now generally recognized as desirable or possible. The fruits of marriage to-day, with all the legal and moral restraints that hedge it about in vain, offer sad confirmation of this position. The time was when freedom in religion was deemed to be dangerous, and the right now enjoyed by so many, with perfect safety to society, to find their religion and their time and place of worship in their own way and choice, was denied and curtailed by church and state. That in some way a freedom for expression of love as between man and woman corresponding to that now enjoyed in religion among many if not all enlightened nations to-day, has been pressed upon the minds of earnest thinkers, each offering limited solution of the problem, but all admitting that unrestrained expression of the impulses of

[1] By Henry James and Stephen Pearl Andrews.

the natural man must be in some way held in equilibrium by the inner or higher powers of the spirit. Deeper and more potent than religious instincts has been the sway of love between man and woman, and by so much more is its right control and directing the greatest essential to their well being individually and socially. Freedom in both religion and love must be within that true service of God, and in accordance with his implanted law, "which alone is perfect freedom," in every direction of life ; a prime requirement being in the underlying principle and safeguard, that none shall exercise their freedom in any direction injuriously to others. A happy illustration of such freedom is shown in the present use of the Christian Sabbath; the rigid observance of which, that once held sway in this community, has gradually yielded to a more enlightened acceptance of the simple words reported of the Master—"The Sabbath was made for man, and not man for the Sabbath."

Very plainly, however, society, with a very few exceptions, has not yet reached the development which would authorize the removal of all bars and restraints in the marriage relation. On the other hand it has been argued that to continue the restraints is a weakening process out of which man would never find his highest manhood. To our mind the truer way is for man to *outgrow* the restraints through a deeper culture of the individual, so that, as before written, the statutes of the State and ordinances of the church shall simply become dead letters, having no application to the social order, and unnecessary in the mouth of magistrate or priest; just as the statutes forbidding great crimes are no longer needed by a large majority of people in every civilized community on earth to-day. With this view in mind, we feel a constant urgency to lay before every intelligent man and woman, the last and best considerations which, after many years of study, have come to us from every source, mundane or spiritual, to help humanity on toward the long promised land which shall be reached by the few at first and later by the many, — the paradise regained, to which no longer the gates with flaming swords will deny admission. Our desire in all this seeking is not for novelty of idea, but for truth, whatever that may be, or however progressed.

Perhaps the foremost thought which

presses itself upon our attention in this regard, is the full recognition of the terrible truth that to *give birth to unwelcome offspring is a crime against humanity!* The full meaning of this needs to be held in the minds and lives of all men and women who are in position possible for parentage. Once taken into their consciousness, both would be so strengthened as to be able to exercise a self-restraint that would be a better safeguard than any statute prohibition. Still more urgent perhaps are the summons to stay that other great wrong, not yet recognized as it should and will be, the crime of infanticide before birth. Man knows not just when the spark of life begins its being as a possible immortal soul. Shutting his eyes to every consideration but his own selfish seeking, he has deemed the stopping of a life only just begun in its lower stages, as a slight if any offence against the laws of God, by which it came into existence! The retribution for such wrong is in the judgment pronounced by the all-Father, in consequences too often attributed to other causes than the real underlying one of selfish seeking. These are plain words, but the times demand them. Too long has the finger been laid upon the lips for hush of inquiry into this most momentous question. False shame of women and underlying selfishness of men have conspired to allow the continuance of old conditions, and the highest and holiest of all social rights been held in cruel bondage. The growing conviction among all who stop to think, that God and nature demand the absolute control of her person by woman in the marriage relation must be established more and more among civilized communities, declared and sustained if need be by statute, until man becomes so subject to the spiritual ruling of his lower instincts and passions, that such statute provision would become unnecessary. The new generations that would come under such ordering would " rise up and call their parentage blessed " indeed, as is now far from being always possible. Children ceasing to be, as they now too often are, creatures of accident and worse, rather than the beautiful fruitage of love under God's law and woman's absolute freedom of person, to which she has a divine right, would no longer have to contend in their growing years with false longings and seeming needs out of inevitable inheritance from the conditions of their con-

ception and birth. Inclinations which now
tend to irritate and preoccupy the minds of
youth, leading and sometimes almost forcing
to indulgence, would no longer divert their
lives from pursuit of higher and worthier
sources of pleasure and growth! It was the
remark in print of a keen observer, that
"man and woman naturally desire each
other, but with this difference; man desires
first, and then loves; whereas woman," as a
rule to which there are sad exceptions from
the conditions of birth, "loves first, and
then desires." It was a beautiful, and as we
believe a just tribute to the average woman;
but a lamentable recognition of the conditions of the average man, resulting directly
from the ruling motive at the time of conception and gestation. Through selfishness
in parentage the lower propensities are naturally predominant in the offspring, and will
continue to be until a purer love moves
both parents with desire only to bless one
another. The world of humanity is crying
out to-day for better conditions of birthright
for every child of man. Would that the
cry could reach the ears of every newly
joined pair, and lead to such recognition of
the awful responsibility in parentage, as

would protect their possible issue from the blight which otherwise awaits them in varying degree, retarding the spirit thus started upon one round of the life immortal. It needs no argument to show that nature forbids indiscriminate mingling of the sexes for selfish purpose. This has been made terribly plain by the consequences sooner or later engendered in such low seeking. Like other sins of man committed in breach of divine law, the punishment is extended to the third and fourth generation from the first evil doer. Communications written through unconscious hands have in years past, and still do respond to earnest inquiries in these inner matters, always confirming the progressive thought toward purer lives and a redeemed humanity.

We have before written that true freedom in love " asserts the right, the bounden duty rather, of woman, to whom the duty first belongs, to protect the fountains of life from every approach that is not actuated by love; and to hold the marriage relation sacred to the cause of parentage, for which it was divinely instituted." This solemn injunction, however, does not mean that parentage is the only purpose and use in marriage ; the interchange of magnetism being always a source of health between man and woman, whether holding the marriage relation or not; and to those holding that relation a continuing source of blessing to both when not stagnated by wasteful use of opportunity. The eyes, the hands, the lips, the presence only offer channels of communication and interchange, and experience has shown to many a happily united pair that these methods will never lose their charm, or cease to bring joy to both so long as the laws of God are obeyed, and selfishness is excluded from all their joining. More and more as these laws are obeyed will the marriage vows hold their efficacy to keep the home what it is at the start in its great purpose, though it be recognized that in the present conditions of earth life the matings are not always the complete union of two souls, which is to be ultimately reached in the joining of the pair ordained of God, the two in one, constituting the complete angel. To this end the promises at the marriage altar are to be kept sacred, with willingness on each part to forget self and keep the home true to those promises; bearing in mind that whatever the ways of man in working up to his highest develop-

ment, true marriage is purely and of necessity monogamic, and to be lived up to in
that conviction. Should this seem sometimes to involve sacrifice on either part, the
blessing that will come of it will surely be
realized ultimately by one if not both.
When men and women have come to a right
understanding of and firm purpose to be
true to divine law, intended to protect every
new-born spirit from contamination, doubtless the interchange of magnetisms may be
sought under the marriage relation, if mutu-
ally desired, through the closest joining
without purpose or thought of parentage.
Woman's absolute control of the situation,
and man's obedience to the law of unselfish-
ness are the essential conditions by which
such communing may be allowed, and bring
its quiet blessing to both. But, as before
written, such happy consummation can
hardly be reached without obedience to the
laws of health in all the appetites of the
physical. Beyond the real needs of health
and strength, indulging his appetite with
meat and drink; living to eat rather than
eating to live, without thought of natural
consequences; man has yielded to the stim-
ulants thus inflaming his lower propensities,

and in the burning of lust, rather than under the prompting of love, he has gone on from generation to generation, handing down the seeds of weakness and ill health, too seldom recognized as the fruits of his ignorance and selfishness. That woman has in a measure shared this lowering of her better nature is not to be denied; but coming last from the hand of God, as the old Scriptures state it, and recognized by man, in her finer instincts as by nature nearer to the divine source of all life, and so more quick to perceive the truth and better able to lead in these momentous questions of the sex relations and parentage, surely she is to be allowed freedom from man's control, exercised through the long centuries; and, thus free, to declare the inner law of her spirit written before man-made statutes were dreamed of.

Years ago it was written through a half unconscious hand, in response to our seeking and inquiry upon this solemn topic, "Your question hath mighty revelations of Light, for it leads into the very beat of the central heart of being, and brings us into those beautiful rays from Light, which are Love, Justice, Charity, Hope and all principles that enter the cells of things and try

to shine through them. God said, " Let
there be Light." Through light and its
uplighting comes immortality. Unless a
man have light in every cell, he is not in
fulness. A dead liver or a dead lung, is
where there is no God. God needs every
cell to uplift itself and light the taper of the
soul." . . . " The Earth is in a low magnetic state. It has not risen above the thermal heat and reds in some of its people ;
while in others there are flames of pure
grade of magnetic power in yellow and blue.
Every mortal or spirit needs the exchange
of the magnetic fires ; for as I told you, all
fires are needed for immortality, and it is
our desire to help mortals to receive these
fires in as high and lofty a grade as possible."

Again it was written, " Do you wonder
that we are trying by all means of principles
instilled into the Earth people to raise the
quality of this rayed light from one to another ? The soul needs it for its roundness
and future immortality. Celibacy is not in
the Divine Law. All things are dual, and
in graded magnetism and electricity, and
God is both Father and Mother ; yet these
fires of exchange must be raised into exceed-
ing finer states than now within the race, or

immortality will require many incarnations. The man never will be immortal without the woman, and vice versa : the one completes the other, and in this completeness the secret of being in God's image lies. No matter at what point comes the exchange of fine threaded light if the quality is pure and white, with delicate pink of affection and tenderness, there will be growth toward immortality. O let us lift them all into these delicate colors, that there shall be no more lust, no more improper longing — no misuse of God's fire! Let us so lift the race that in the closest exchanges there may be the white fire only without its material shield : for the highest angels do exchange by the white fire, and not by the low thermal state of heat. I say all beings need the blending of one soul in another. It is the mother mingling with the father — or the sphering of the two in one, representing God and the Son and the fire or the Holy Ghost ; these being the holy Trinity in which all is. No man can be celibate and become in fulness, for he would lack the mother flame or the illumined God. We bid you preach these truths ! "

Various forms of the free love doctrine

have seemed to come in with the other claims for freedom of thought and action, under the promptings of the mediums of Modern Spiritualism. But surely this does not mean wild license; the freedom which soon kills itself by wanton indulgence and perhaps most selfish encroachment upon the rights of others. It means rather liberation from the bonds which have heretofore, in man's slow development, seemed necessary to protect the marriage relation and the sacredness of the home circles, and are yet far from useless with too many who could not bear any loosening of the bonds without danger of results that would be ruinous to the best social order. This liberation can safely come only through growth of the individual toward that highest aim of the deepest thinkers, when each, by development of soul culture and the God that is within all, can become a law unto themselves. The freedom then will be not in liberation from the external restraint, but in the subjection of the lower nature to the spiritual life of every man and woman; not crushing the lower nature, but so sustained in the higher and spiritual, that the lower will come into action only when and as prompted by the

higher. Then it will be true for both man
and woman, and not for woman only, as
before quoted, to "love first and then desire "; — never the reverse. Is it expecting
too much of man and woman as they now
average, to reach this standpoint? We can
only say that it never will be reached unless
"the mark of the prize of the high calling"
be held up before them, till gradually all
may be drawn to its wonderful and beautiful
possibilities by an attraction that will as it
were compel obedience to the divine law
implanted in every human being to be
worked out into joyful fruition.

It was a beautiful inspiration that wrote, —

"O Truth, I love thee ; it were sweet to pass
Into thy essence, as a globe of glass,
Melted and shivered by intensest light
To flow and mingle with thy Infinite.
O Truth, O Monarch, O thou conquering God,
Would that I were a meadow violet trod
Beneath thy feet, to feel thy Godhood thrill
This dust, this me, then lie forever still !
Nay, nay thy touch should make me turn to fire ;
I'd rise transformed from Nature's funeral pyre,
Echoing thy thought. — Alas, alas, how weak,
How utter weak: — the hot blood burns my cheek:
My aspirations are for thee ; my life,
Like a fallen tear drop in cold seas of strife

Sinks down — the exhaling tear ascends above
The eyes that wept it forth ; — I feel Thy love,
O loving Spirit, and this tear, this me,
A star of soul becomes informed by Thee."

Let no one argue that plain treatment and
unveiling of the momentous interests involved in the marriage relation might disturb
the peace, or possibly give false direction to
the thoughts of young men or women, whose
minds have been entirely free from the " lep-
rosy of sensual thought or desire." To such
minds ignorance is not bliss when they are
brought, as in the course of nature they may
and should be, into position where want of
knowledge is a snare into which many an
innocent young woman, and some young
men have been led under cover of the marriage rites as usually construed, despite their
own native consciousness that all is not conducted as it should be. Light, more light
is demanded for each and all who are likely
sooner or later to be brought into possible
relations of parentage ; for the man, that he
shall not ignorantly and selfishly intrude
himself upon the woman; and for the woman
that she may guard sacredly the high and
holy calling of maternity, through intelligent

co-operation with the laws implanted by the All-Father in her organism for the preservation and improvement of the race.

To those whose lives are already infected with more or less seeming need and desire, arising sadly out of the conditions of their birth under selfish promptings, rather than the love which God meant should be the actuating motive, such inquiry into the laws of true marriage-life will prove helpful and sustaining in the struggles with self, and in the end lift them to a higher plane, quite above such seeming need. It would lead them to recognize that the lower promptings have their use when all the higher conditions are satisfied, so that passion given expression under the moving sanction of love, shall bring all the forces of the natural man into co-operation with the spiritual man; and thus every new born spirit, while yet in embryo, can rightly take on its leading conditions, to be unfolded through experience on the earth plane. Gradually, it is to be hoped, man will rise to this higher calling, partly through better culture and ruling of the daily life, but more through better parentage in which all the rest is practically involved. Let these injunctions be accepted and lived up

to as fast and as far as increasing knowledge
and higher aspirations for the truth of God
make possible, and in good time will the
earth blossom and rejoice with a regenerated
humanity, such as now can only be anticipated with a divine hope. Then and not
till then will woman's servitude be looked
back upon as a terrible dream of a long and
weary past; and men and women meeting
together shall be as children of God, always
strong in true manhood and womanhood,
through their mutual obedience to his law.
Then may be realized the beautiful promise
of the poet from whose inspiration we have
already quoted, —

" There is a world whose multitudinous race
One God inspires; through every human face
Beams forth the mild Divinity of Love;
Their forms are beautiful and pure above
All mortal knowledge. There my soul was led
In solemn vision, and an Angel said,
' Explore these bright dominions, treasure well
In spirit-consciousness the miracle,
The wonder and the glory thou shalt see;
As that orb is, thy orb is yet to be."

God speed the time and its fulfilment.
He will, but through man's development
and beautiful obedience to the laws of true

life. It can be reached in no other way. To repeat, we claim that beyond controversy : I. Woman must never yield her person to man out of selfish purpose, but always with desire rather to bless. II. She must be free to decide when and under what conditions she may seek to become a mother. On this point man must be absolutely submissive. III. Man must be lifted out of selfish purpose in all his approaches, and rejoice in perfect freedom from subjection to his own lower nature. Such is the freedom which the higher angels would help man and woman to achieve. It is the corner-stone in the foundation of that kingdom which is to come on earth as in heaven. From generation to generation, down the long line of ancestry, the blessing in fulfilment of these requirements may be transmitted. The planet waits for something better in the new order now opening for all the forces of nature. It will be a revelation, indeed, when this development under a true Christian civilization is reached ; and those solemn words of the Master, uttered nearly two thousand years ago, " he that looketh upon a woman with desire that is not born of love, committeth the forbidden sin," shall be an effective

substitute for the statute law now vainly endeavoring through threat of punishment to
suppress the secret wrongs hidden from the
public eye, and too often sadly committed
under cover of the marriage certificate.

For many years these thoughts have been
pressing upon our mind. In early youth
a deep compassion for women who had fallen
into servitude to man's selfishness moved
the writer with earnest desire, now partially
fulfilled in these writings, to do what he could
to meet and help overcome the terrible social
evil. Similar thoughts have found expression through divers other sources among
truth seeking men and women. But not till
now has the fulness of time seemed to call
for such free expression, or been ready to
welcome an open consideration of this momentous topic of the sex relations. With
earnest prayer that the work of redemption
may soon be taken up and carried to its ultimate, long hoped for results, we leave it in
His hands for whom we would ever labor in
loving service !

Plain words have been written ! May
they quicken the perceptions of men to recognize, and strengthen the native instinct
and promptings of woman to insist upon her

divine right and bounden duty to be a free agent in the exercise of her calling under God to give birth only to offspring worthy to be accepted as his children! Would not the parentage of the Christ man fail of its great teaching, if it did not illustrate the possibilities of true Motherhood, as an ultimate attainment of all true Womanhood? Has not the time come for such recognition here and now, whenever and wherever a human eye rests upon these pages?

Father, may our life in Thee
Be hid through all Eternity !
By Love inspired, by Wisdom taught,
Be all our action, all our thought
Forever to Thy service brought,
In true humility !

APPENDIX

THE following statement, gathered from most reliable sources, will be of interest to the general reader.

The First Spiritual Temple, so-called because the first of its kind in modern times, was completed in 1885. It is a beautiful stone structure, covering an area of eighty-four by one hundred and ten feet; the main auditorium having a seating capacity for fifteen hundred persons. It was erected at a cost of two hundred and fifty thousand dollars, and rivals in architectural effect, after its kind, some of the most costly of the many places of worship in the city of Boston. Very nearly the whole cost was met out of an accumulation from successful business, by one man, whose deep interest carried the work to completion, and who has since held the chief place in its direction, and in large measure borne its current expenses. By a deed of Trust it was placed, and still stands in the name of three Trustees, of whom the builder is the chief, with ample power to maintain the uses declared. It was dedicated on the evenings of September 26th, 27th and 28th, 1885, under the auspices of the Spiritual Fraternity, the name given to the Society attending its ministrations.

In the deed of Trust it is declared that "this Tem-

ple is to be used for the promulgation of principles
which shall inculcate the highest moral good for humanity.   All isms which shall tend to warp or dis-
tort the spirit, or which shall place the intelligence
of the people under any bonds, shall be excluded
from its teachings.   A temperate attitude toward all
the great questions of the day and all civic questions
under the law pertaining to the general moral good,
shall be strictly maintained."   . . .   " All dogmas,
creeds or rituals interfering with progressive thought
shall be excluded.   It shall be devoted to the promulgation of spiritual truths through the highest intelligences, whether embodied or disembodied.   It
is devoted to enlighten conscience, to give liberty of
thought, without license of speech."

At the consecration service held in the Temple on
the evening of September 26th, in the presence of
fifty-seven persons, a spirit, later known as The Temple Spirit, materialized through the help of a well-
known medium in a curtained apartment or cabinet,
placed for the purpose, upon the platform of the
main auditorium.   Appearing outside at first like a
column of phosphorescent light by the altar, at
length the outlines of a human form, arrayed in a
peculiar luminous robe, with a tall head-dress or
mitre as luminous, were dimly visible.

After repeatedly advancing and retreating toward
the cabinet, as if to gain strength, the Spirit de-
scended to the floor of the auditorium.   As he came
near, his extended robe was seen to be composed of
the finest lace, possessing a singular luminosity,
while an under garment resembling velvet, of a rich
purple color, on which were figures of apparently
symbolic character, was visible.   After reaching the

floor and passing up the nearest aisle and down another, a distance of over two hundred feet, he partly reascended the platform steps, whence he addressed, in low whispers, several persons called from the audience for the purpose. Then gaining strength through the aid of a powerful voice-medium, he addressed the whole assembly in tones loud enough to be heard throughout the auditorium; closing with these words —

"I consecrate this Temple to holy living,— to universal brotherhood, — to the cultivation of that spirit which the Divine Master brought with him in his life and teachings on earth, — to unity of the spiritual life with that on earth, that there may be but one life, one brotherhood, one God and Father of us all, —that from this place may be taught that wisdom which shall recognize more than teachings from the intellect, even the development and wisdom of heart-life; that here the hearts of people may be awakened *to do*, as well as their heads *to think*, for only through the wisdom that comes from both heart and head can God be brought near to help us in all our endeavors. And may all who come to listen have receptive hearts to be taught how to live the divine life — Amen."

On the following evening a public dedication took place before a crowded audience; and on the evening of September 28th, a Dedicatory Festival was held.

Besides the large auditorium, the Temple contains a smaller Audience room and a Library room below, with minor offices; and in the upper story has seven small Audience rooms, capable of holding from one to four hundred persons.

As intimated in the preceding pages of this book, adverse influences seem to have retarded the work anticipated at the dedication of the Temple ; but nothing has yet occurred to render impossible the ultimate fulfilment of all its early hopes and promises.

Some interesting Articles by Pres. A. D. White, Cornell, were published a few years since, giving a brief outline of the treatment of insane people from the early days, when they were often held in chains and otherwise cruelly treated, to the modern gentle methods, and as far as possible freedom from restraint, now generally recognized as the wiser as well as kinder treatment. The Articles referred to would have been more intelligently written and more helpful, if their writer had been more familiar with the facts of Modern Spiritualism, and especially with the subject of spirit "Obsession," briefly treated in this book.

THE END.

MANUFACTURED BY CUPPLES & SCHOENHOF,
BOSTON, U. S. A.

BOOKS OF VALUE
AND INTEREST

Issued by

Cupples & Schoenhof

BOSTON

Hiero-Salem; or, the Vision of Peace.

Being a Fiction founded on Ideals which are grounded in the Real, that is greater than the greatest of all Human Great Ideals. By EVELEEN LAURA MASON.

With 9 Illustrations.

This lengthy, intricate and elaborate novel has sorely puzzled the ordinary critic ! Nevertheless the book must delight those interested in the uncommon paths of literature, especially in Buddhism, Theosophy, and the Position of Woman,— but more particularly in the Androgynous idea, *i.e.* the dual-sex mental philosophy mentioned by Coleridge. The late Parker Pillsbury pronounced Mrs. Mason the cleverest woman in America.

In 1 vol. square octavo. 508 pages, cloth. $2.00 *net.*

Above mailed, postage paid, to any address, on receipt of price.

Cupples & Schoenhof, Publishers, Boston.